SHE THROWS HERSELF
FORWARD
TO STOP THE FALL

STORIES BY
DAVE NEWMAN

ROADSIDE PRESS

Cover Art: Lou Ickes
Editor: Michele McDannold

Roadside Press
Colchester, Illinois

For Jakiela, upside down and sideways
Thank you, thank you, thank you

Contents

Suddenly I realize
that if I stepped out of my body
I would break into blossom
–James Wright

I had no choice, I had to make good
–John Fante

CAPTAIN POEM AND THE PART-TIMER'S REVOLT

Bonnie needs to call the landlord and she needs to sound successful or confident or hard-working or however a woman hiding bad credit needs to sound to get into an apartment without having the landlord know she's fucked up everything there is to fuck up when it comes to money and paying it back on time.

Bonnie plunks down at the dining room table to think.

It's morning, early.

Bonnie's mom says, "Honey, you should just take today off."

Bonnie says, "I can't, Mom."

"I'll buy lunch."

"Thanks, I still can't."

"You're no fun," Bonnie's mom says, gathering up her purse.

Bonnie's mom is a medical secretary. She used to bartend at a fancy restaurant by the hospital until one of the doctors, drunk and happy, begged her to join his team. Bonnie's mom thought the doctor was another horny rich guy but he paid her a bonus when she started and now she works four days a week and makes good money.

Bonnie teaches basic writing at five different colleges, cobbling together full-time employment from part-time jobs.

Her mom says, "You work too hard."

"I do," Bonnie says, not arguing.

Yesterday, after her night class, Bonnie stopped at Sheetz and put twelve dollars of gas in her tank. The gauge stayed on empty, only tweaking the line going downhill. She drove home, maybe using half a gallon. At home she called the landlord but the landlord's hearing was nearly gone. He sounded like a cannonball victim. Bonnie raised her voice. It didn't matter. She thought about her car and gas and how far she needed to drive.

"Call whenever," he said. "I'm almost always up."

Bonnie was so tired.

The fifty papers stuffed in her bag needed to be corrected a week earlier.

The landlord said, "You want directions?"

Bonnie said she did.

He gave her directions.

He said, "Call whenever."

The landlord cleared his throat, spit, and hung up.

Bonnie wrote the landlord's number and the apartment's address on a scrap of paper. Her purse was filled with scraps of paper, things to do that wouldn't get done.

She wished she still owned a phone.

* * *

Bonnie is thirty-nine but tells people she is thirty-six.

Five years ago she moved home for a couple weeks while she waited to move somewhere else, a one-bedroom rental in Ligonier, not far from Saint Francis where she taught sometimes, but the landlord charged her for a credit check and submitted the credit check and the credit people denied her application.

The weeks extended.

Her mom said, "I'm so happy you're home!"

Bonnie had stacked her life neatly against her mom's garage wall, hoping not to unpack, hoping to fill another rental truck and drive to another rental space, but on weekends she pulled various items from various boxes then quit pulling and brought everything into the bedroom, her old bedroom. She locked the door and unscrewed a bottle of wine then opened boxes all evening. She ripped tape. She pulled flaps. She started with make-up and clothes then dug out her haircare products then her music then her little TV. Pretty soon she had an old photograph of Jean Rhys she loved tacked to the wall above her desk. Jean Rhys wrote like a genius made of booze, a genius made of privilege and failure. Jean Rhys had fucked a lot of powerful guys, hoping for success. She wrote great stories set in old hotels and worse bars.

Bonnie hoped to become Jean Rys without becoming Jean Rhys.

Bonnie wanted the grit but not the pain.

Bonnie splurged and bought a desk lamp for twelve dollars at a yard sale and shined it on whatever she read at night, mostly student papers, sometimes still books.

Her mom said, "You're a great roommate."

Her mom said, "You should work less."

Her mom said, "We could have lunch on Mondays."

Bonnie checked out other rentals, sometimes two in one evening, and she read the real estate sites religiously, but suddenly the landlords all looked like they would run credit checks when it used to be they looked like grandparents handing out candy. Bonnie wrote down more addresses and toured more apartments and taught more classes and kept believing she'd save money by living at home.

There was no money to save.

The money she makes teaching classes is never enough to make her look like someone who teaches classes. She wears outfits from years ago and can feel her tiny gut press against the waistbands of old pants even though she has lost weight. For the one job she interviewed for last year, she carefully removed the tags from a dress she bought at H&M then carefully hooked the tags back on before she returned it.

In July Bonnie will be forty, years past the age of living at home. Her mom is sweet and understanding and considerate and encouraging but encouraging to the point of bullying, to the point of diminishing. There are not enough walls to separate their dreams. Her mom says, "Write a book like Stephen King!" Her mom says, "Write a book like that John Grisham!" She says, "Write a mystery that starts with the letter Q!" Her mom reads Danielle Steele books and says, "People like romance novels," and she says, "Write for the movies!" and she says, "Write for TV!" like TV and movie people are everywhere, desperate for writers, desperate for Bonnie. Her mom says, "I bet a lot of cute men write for the movies."

Bonnie seldom watches movies anymore because she does not date, because she is so busy with teaching, because movies remind her she owes money on things that no longer exist. Blockbuster Video, out of business for a decade, still wants their money back.

Last night, from her childhood bed, Bonnie heard her mother in the other room watching a TV movie called *The Last Loves of Lila James* on one of the women's networks. Lila James was a desperate woman but men appeared to be attracted to Lila's desperation and Bonnie resented that. "You don't need to live like this, Lila," a man said in a strong voice and Lila started to weep

Fuck you, Lila James, Bonnie thought.

Now it's morning.

Bonnie sits in her car, shuffling a pile of student papers.

Last night, sleep and exhaustion became separate things, opposites, until exhaustion worked against sleep and became anxiety, until Bonnie promised herself she would rise early, in the four o'clock hour, until she closed her eyes and counted how many pages she corrected last semester, around three thousand, until she opened her eyes and sat up and forced herself to breathe, until Lila James in the other room finally found the right love and Bonnie's mom turned off the TV and Bonnie listened to her mom's slippers shuffling.

Now Bonnie stays in her car until she feels weird about being in her car.

* * *

Her 8:30 Comp II is upstairs. The part-time office sits in the basement and is not really an office but a closety room made of cinderblocks and old tinted glass with three chairs and one desk for five part-time English professors. No pictures or paintings or inspirational messages hang on the walls. One of the three chairs wobbles.

The time is 8:05.

The university—a branch campus with twelve-hundred mostly commuter students—is quiet and echoes Bonnie's steps. She walks on, feeling outside her life.

Bonnie waves at the secretaries behind the glass in their oversized office. They wave back. Bonnie loves the secretaries. They put out brownies or cookies on Fridays for the part-time faculty and allow Bonnie extra copies when her copy limit has been exceeded.

One of the secretaries opens the glass and says, "Almost Friday!"

It's only Wednesday.

Bonnie says, "I love your optimism," and she does.

In the classroom Bonnie puts down her bag. No students have arrived yet. The lights are off and it feels like evening. Bonnie misses evenings. Before she started teaching college, she worked as a bartender and a waitress then started picking up night classes no one else wanted. She last held a job where she ate dinner at dinner time, sitting down and not in her car or standing in a kitchen or behind a bar, when she was in graduate school, almost half her life ago. Bonnie misses dinner. She misses breakfast. She misses vacations.

She misses so much, everything.

She hates when her mind bends to desires she cannot afford.

Are there people left who can afford their desires?

Bonnie thinks there must be but she does not know them.

A boy-student Bonnie doesn't recognize walks into the classroom, looks around like he has stepped from an escalator into a women's clothing store, and says, "Wrong class."

Bonnie says, "The semester is almost over."

The student says, "I know," and walks out.

Bonnie wishes she had her cell phone to call the landlord but her cell phone disappeared two years ago, the bill at a collection agency where so many of her bills have ended up.

She can't believe she uses her mom's landline.

She can't believe her mom has a landline.

Right after finishing her undergraduate degree, when she would have taken any job where she could have pretended to use her education, Bonnie charged up business suits and ugly shoes and a goofy briefcase with a strap, never imagining her Mastercard would come due and she wouldn't have a career where she could use the things she'd charged. So she charged more. And more. Even Bonnie's face is in debt. She owes almost eight hundred dollars on her Sephora card, which she pays the interest on every month, because her skin breaks out when she uses cheap make-up and she can't afford to get her face medicine because her dermatologist charges a sixty-five dollar co-pay and her insurance is the cheapest available.

Bonnie gets her hair cut at the community college.

She hasn't seen her gynecologist in years.

She could go to the free clinic and be embarrassed and park across the street in the Pizza Hut parking lot and see a strange gynecologist but Bonnie does not want to be in the same room where abortions are performed on teenage girls, no offense to the teenage girls.

Out in the hall someone calls her name. Then again, only louder. By the third call Bonnie recognizes the voice as Vincent Colosimo, one of the tenured faculty members.

Bonnie picks up her book bag and thinks of bolting for the ladies restroom, somewhere Vincent Colosimo will not enter. "I have my period!" she'd like to shout at Vincent Colosimo but of course Bonnie does not have her period, she does not even know when her period is due, she cannot summon her period like a coat of armor, and thank god her mom got knocked up with Bonnie at thirteen years old and still sometimes menstruates or spots or whatever her mom calls it because Bonnie cannot afford tampons.

Bonnie grabs her keys and steps into the hall. Vincent Colosimo has passed her room, walking away. She moves in the opposite direction. Her heels clack. Vincent turns. He calls. She pretends his voice is a student calling another student, some other Bonnie.

He says, "Bonnie, wait!"

Bonnie glances and waves but does not stop.

Vincent is fat and short, bowling-ball'ish from neck to dick. Skinny legs prop up his roundness like toothpicks in a meatball. His arms are long and devoid of muscle. The long salt-and-pepper hair he pulls back in a ponytail swishes from side to side when he hustles along the halls. He wears sandals with socks. Bonnie knows Vincent Colosimo cannot catch her if she runs. Sandals. Gut. Skinny legs. But she does not want to run.

Running is defeat.

His footsteps pick up, sandals flapping.

She keeps going, reminding herself that she needs to call the landlord. An apartment awaits her. Hopefully. She is not running from Vincent Colosimo but running to a better future.

Vincent, low on breath and volume, coughs Bonnie's name.

She thinks he will quit and find her later.

Vincent will go to his office and make a poem.

Vincent does that.

He is a poet and he makes poems, weekly, maybe daily, and he likes to recite these poems because he believes people have lost touch with the oral tradition of poetry. Vincent does readings, sometimes on campus. He invites everyone, all his colleagues, especially the part-time faculty who cannot say no to the full-time faculty because full-time faculty may somehow someday have hiring power and part-time faculty want to be hired full-time.

"Bonnie!" Vincent shouts, mustering air.

Bonnie does not run towards Vincent, shouting about herself, ever.

She would not do this to anyone, ever.

She corners down the next hall.

One of the secretaries, Anna, turns from the soda machine.

Anna says, "Run faster," and laughs.

"I'm trying," Bonnie says. "I feel like a jerk."

She says, "I'll stall him. Keep going."

Bonnie says, "Thank you," and makes it through the double doors and down the stairs and heads for the phone from another decade.

She stops outside the door, out of breath like she'd caught obesity from Vincent Colosimo's voice, from his clumsy steps, like the worries that haunt her brain have jumped and turned her lungs into a trampoline. She flips through her keychain, speeding through keys that open doors at five different schools and a half-dozen more keys she's never returned from other colleges where she's taught.

Bonnie looks at her keys and says, "Shit."

For a minute she does not hear Vincent, Vincent whose success shames her, Vincent whose success is not success, Vincent who says things like, "I currently have a manuscript under consideration for the very prestigious Flannery O'Connor Prize," when the Flannery O'Connor Prize is a contest that charges reading fees and accepts submissions from anyone with twenty-five dollars, including students and gas station attendants.

Bonnie finds the right key but stops before she can open the door.

Vincent steps around the corner and says, "You didn't hear me calling."

Bonnie says, "I'm totally out of it in the morning," and tries to look confused, sleep-deprived but still functional, which is like an actress playing an actress in a film about acting.

Vincent says, "I've been trying to talk to everyone in the department," and he motions like the entire department is present.

A bead of sweat rolls from his forehead.

Vincent sweats so much but does not smell. Bonnie wishes he smelled awful, like old tuna and dog shit and garbage cans. It'd be another way to warn the world.

Vincent says, "Allow me a second to get my air. I apologize."

"Sure," Bonnie says, hoping his air will not get.

* * *

Years ago Bonnie approached the department chair about teaching a poetry class instead of all composition courses. Bonnie had never requested anything. Part-time faculty accepted what was offered. She found him in the hallway outside his office. She made her pitch and he was not openly hostile. He nodded. He leaned.

He said, "Sounds interesting."

The department chair never wore a tie. He thought this made him more accessible. Maybe it did. He'd seen the Grateful Dead in 1978 in Pittsburgh, his last year in graduate school. He'd played in a band that opened for the Ramones.

Bonnie said, "I've taught poetry before, at other schools, and I've published a lot," and she started to list a few journals where her poems had been accepted.

He said, "Sounds like you're doing your work."

Suddenly, Vincent appeared.

He lifted his hand in a dramatic gesture and said, "First, an original composition," then recited a short poem about his great uncle bringing the family spaghetti sauce recipe from Italy. The last stanza said, "the best sauce from the boot / starts from the olives / grown in the heel" and Vincent closed his eyes like he'd finished a prayer.

Then he handed them a flier for his upcoming reading.

The department chair said, "Spaghetti sauce in a poem—who knew?"

Vincent said, "If you two could just share this because I'm running out of fliers."

Vincent walked off without saying goodbye or thank-you.

The department chair, not even pretending to be impressed, shook his head.

He turned to Bonnie and said, "There goes Captain Poem," and, before Bonnie could agree or disagree, he added, "What a self-promotional asshole."

Bonnie shook her head too but not much, not enough.

The department chair said, "When's your next class?"

Bonnie looked at her watch and said, "Soon."

He said, "Me too," and walked off.

Their discussion could have ended better, admittedly, but Bonnie assumed the department chair understood her, that something could happen, that creative classes, or at least a creative class, were imminent, but Bonnie also wondered why the department chair had given Vincent tenure and attended his awful readings and why he was paying her seventeen hundred dollars to teach a summer class when Vincent made five times as much money.

She never got the poetry class.

She never asked again.

* * *

Back at the part-time office Vincent finds his air and says, "Those stairs kill me."

Vincent had a heart attack, a small one, five years ago.

Bonnie thinks about it, the clutched chest, the job opening.

Vincent says, "I have a new book coming out and I'm trying to get a big sendoff. If everyone teaches the book, it will really unify the campus, pedagogically speaking."

Bonnie says, "Great, good. Send me the flier, the info, the email. Whatever you end up sending, just send it to me." She says, "I'll read it."

Vincent says, "That sounds like a confirmation," but his expression barely changes, the glassed eyes still glassy. "The library does something now where they sponsor one book and encourage the entire community to read it. People don't realize that poetry, like language itself, holds value in any classroom and out in the world. Librarians should know this most of all."

Bonnie shrugs.

Vincent keeps talking—language, poetry, his book, support.

He says, "This isn't as food-centric as my last book of poems or as interested in geography as my fiction but, of course, there are elements of those two themes in the new collection. Just as Pound's *Cantos* was an extension of his earlier work."

It's like a skit, a spoof.

Bonnie wants to nod her head: you're fucking kidding me.

But maybe Vincent Colosimo is mentally ill, brain sick, maybe he is autistic or stuck with a personality disorder he can't control or isn't even conscious of. Bonnie reaches out and touches his cheek as if brushing away a piece of lint or offering him all the tenderness in her fingers but Vincent does not respond, not even a twitch.

His eyebrows are so bushy they look like shrubs lining an abandoned house.

Bonnie wonders what she would look like if she quit, if she gave up on all of it, the plucking and shaving, the showering, talking sense.

Would there be rewards?

Bonnie imagines stabbing herself in the neck with a small pen knife.

"I'm fine," she'd tell Vincent, "please don't stop the bleeding."

Now Vincent says, "I'm excited to have you on board."

Bonnie cannot teach Vincent Colosimo's book because she knows it is self-absorbed bullshit and yet she must teach Vincent Colosimo's book if she wants her dreams to be anything more than overdue bills so she will put Vincent Colosimo's book on her syllabus and the students will buy it but they will get behind that semester and Bonnie will not teach the book which the students have paid for and is on her syllabus.

Sorry students, tough shit.

* * *

Years ago Bonnie taught a self-published Vincent Colosimo book. She assigned it and read it and made notes in the margins then she lectured on it, saying as many positive things as she could, things that contradicted all the rules and lectures and criteria for good writing she'd delivered all semester. She blushed while teaching. She quit her lecture when her neck felt on-fire.

One student said, "Is this a joke?"

Bonnie said, "What?"

The student said, "O holy sausage?"

Bonnie said, "Well."

Another student said, "Heaven is not an anchovy pizza, sorry."

A third student said, "What is wrong with this guy?"

The first student said, "Does he actually believe this shit?"

Bonnie said, "Let's try to be more generous."

One of her students, one time, maybe last semester, maybe last year, asked Vincent Colosimo for a letter of recommendation and Vincent Colosimo responded by asking the student to write a letter on Vincent's behalf and submit it to the dean.

The student said, "Is that normal?"

The student said, "All he does is teach 'The Egg' and talk about himself." The student said, "Sherwood Anderson fucking sucks."

Bonnie said, "I like Sherwood Anderson," but she didn't, not really.

* * *

Vincent says, "One of the blurbs I'm looking to acquire will say: tour de force," and he holds up the imaginary letters like the blurb is a marquee.

Bonnie thinks: the blurb I'm looking to acquire?

Bonnie is looking to acquire the Pulitzer Prize right after she acquires some sort of employment that provides enough income to eat a take-out burrito.

This goes on because Vincent wills it to go on.

Bonnie, completely lapsing, says, "Why do you self-publish your books?"

Vincent says, "I do not think of them as self-published."

Bonnie thinks one of them was maybe not self-published.

It was maybe published by his wife.

He said the new one had a publisher.

She thought she heard that.

Bonnie puts her hand on Vincent's shoulder and squeezes so he can't ignore the touch. Vincent looks at her face like someone who has been told the importance of eye-contact but still can't locate the eyes. Maybe the job turned Vincent this way. Maybe Bonnie does not want a full-time teaching job because a full-time teaching job will take her mind.

Bonnie says, "I'm sorry. I really need to make a phone call."

Vincent says, "You can get a teacher's copy directly from me for ten dollars."

Bonnie says, "I thought teachers' copies were free."

"No," Vincent says. "Not in this instance," and walks away.

* * *

Bonnie does not call the landlord. She would like to cancel class but she needs to save her next cancel for when she wakes up and cannot stop weeping. She leaves the part-time office.

She walks the hall, worried about being spotted.

She finds a room filled with students.

She teaches until she realizes almost no one has read the assignment.

She says, "And now for the quiz," and hands out a quiz she had no intention of giving out but had printed up in case the classes hadn't read the material.

It takes a while but the students start writing and finish the quiz. They drop their quizzes face down on her table, nod politely, and leave.

She waits, relieved to not be teaching.

A freshman with dyed black hair and chipped

black fingernails slowly finishes the quiz. His blue jeans are bleached out and partly shredded and he's cute in the way that sad boys sometimes are. Sad kids used to be goth then they turned emo. Goth kids wrote essays about killing others. Emo kids wrote essays about killing themselves. This kid writes about deer hunting with his dad and uncles when he writes at all.

The boy hands in his quiz and sulks away.

Bonnie looks at the quiz and calls his name.

The kid turns slightly and stretches his bangs into his eyes and tugs at his collar. Bonnie holds up the quiz. The quiz is blank.

Bonnie says, "You could guess."

He shrugs and messes his hair.

She says, "Are you sure? You could make some stuff up on the essay and get partial credit. I'm a pretty easy grader."

He says, "I guess I'm okay," and turns to leave.

Bonnie says, "Read the text then ask for a make-up quiz?"

"Probably not," he says, and walks off.

Only Jeffrey, the best writer in the class, remains.

Jeffrey says, "Sorry, I'm almost done," and goes back to the quiz, erasing marks.

Bonnie says, "Take your time," but means the opposite.

Jeffrey is too smart for this quiz, which is open-book and open-note. If he didn't read anything but still glanced at the syllabus, he could pass. Jeffrey chews his pencil. He turns the paper over and starts to write then stops writing.

Bonnie says, "You're allowed to skip one quiz. If you didn't get a chance to read the text, it's not a big deal."

"No, I read it," Jeffrey says and smiles.

Bonnie goes back to *Without Stopping*, a Paul Bowles memoir. She knows little about Bowles and this book and its convoluted writing only adds to the confusion. Bowles lives in Tangiers. The peasants are beautiful. The drugs are cheap. The food is cheap. People buy cafes. People sell cafes. Hip writers come for visits. Here's Tennessee Williams trying to lay young Moroccan men. Here's William Burroughs shooting dope. Here's Allen Ginsberg being Allen Ginsberg. Here's Jack Kerouac, drunk. Here's Bowles again, watching. Then the writing crumbles into itself, a big black hole of nothingness.

Jeffrey says, "I'm sorry this is taking so long."

Bonnie says, "Less apology, more quiz," but makes it sound happy.

She'd read another Paul Bowles book, *The Spider's House*, and it bored her too. She liked *The Sheltering Sky* but she'd been a grad student and lots of people in workshop were reading Bowles. One of her peers said, "I believe there's a Bowles renaissance going on as we speak." That was grad school. No one read to read. They read to talk. A rich white girl tried writing a novel in the voice of a slave. Their white male professor told her that was appropriation.

Everyone in class cried.

Jeffrey finishes the quiz and walks to the front of the room.

Bonnie says, "Done?"

He says, "I'm sorry, two more minutes," and hustles back to his seat.

Bonnie sometimes wonders how it is at real colleges, big colleges, universities where the students don't work full-time or hold two jobs or drive to campus in rusted-out trucks, universities where the students' parents help with tuition and everyone is not saddled with fifty grand in loans. She imagines those kids studying all the time.

She imagines they're boring as hell.

Bonnie used to dream of teaching graduate students at a major university, which is what she called it, a major university, and now she wishes she could keep working at this branch campus but fulltime because she loves these students, these kids who work at Walmart and wait tables in sports bars. She knows she qualifies for food stamps, which are not called food stamps anymore, they call them something fancy, vouchers maybe, but she cannot bring herself to fill out the application. She looks at Jeffrey.

She says, "You doing okay?"

Jeffrey stands and says, "Here's my test, I apologize."

He is not as handsome as the sad boy but he looks more grown up and less practiced with his buzzed hair and jeans and polo shirt. He seldom shaves so his cheeks are lightly fuzzed. Jeffrey looks like a young man, earnest and hard-working and filled with dreams, something Bonnie seldom sees anymore because most of her students turn from kids to adults without a pitstop of hope, their bad college jobs becoming their first real jobs then their careers.

Bonnie says, "How'd you do?"

"Good," he says. "I just wanted to nail the essay question."

"I'm sure you nailed it," she says.

Jeffrey looks at the floor.

Bonnie knows what that means. Jeffrey needs a letter of recommendation. He needs a tutor. He needs a friend, a counselor. He is suicidal. He is gay. He has been recently dumped. His girlfriend is pregnant. He is alone. He is alive and it hurts.

Jeffrey finishes his downward stare and says, "The reason I'm hanging around is because I really like you. I appreciate what you do and I wanted to see if maybe we could have a beer or a cup of coffee sometime. You're great. I'm not like a stalker or anything."

"That's so sweet," Bonnie says, syrupy, a little too flattered. "You're the best student I've had in a long time." She pauses. She knows what she wants to say but not how. "You're great but it wouldn't be appropriate for me to go out with you."

Jeffrey says, "Oh, okay."

Bonnie says, "No big deal."

Bonnie never dates students, though she knows people, lots of them, usually tenured professors, who do date students. She tries not to judge those people, though she does, she judges them, because students are students and it would be gross to bang one, a kid who forgets to turn in their paper on time or flunks open-book exams.

Jeffrey says, "I'm embarrassed."

Bonnie says, "Don't be."

Jeffrey says, "I think I misspoke," but not embarrassed, more confused. "I didn't mean a date like a date. I didn't mean a date at all."

Bonnie says, "Don't apologize," but she knows he's not apologizing.

He says, "What?"

The only thing worse than being hit on by students is not being hit on by students or imagining you're being hit on by a student who is not hitting on you.

Bonnie says, "I think you misunderstood what I was saying. I mean, in general," and she feels like a total asshole.

Jeffrey says, "You teach a great class."

Bonnie says, "Thanks."

The Vice President at this campus—a fifty-seven-year-old man with dyed-black hair who wears short-shorts and plays tennis exclusively with female students—bangs both his middle-aged secretary and a girl on student government who carries around a pink gym bag with a pink racquet sticking out.

Jeffrey says, "This is the best class I've taken all year."

Bonnie imagines herself fucking the Vice President, doing it for a job, for a raise or a promotion, an image flying across her brain-screen.

Jeffrey says, "I'm pretty much a gentleman. My mom raised me that way."

Bonnie says, "I'm sure, I'm just really in a hurry."

Jeffrey says, "I took some years off after high school. I'm almost twenty-four. I've been working shit jobs—construction, bartending, a road crew in Alabama during the middle of the summer—and I want to make the right choice when it comes to picking a major. I need to get a good job when I'm done here. My dad works as a mechanic. We didn't have much growing up."

"Sure," Bonnie says. "I'd be happy to help," but she can only help by example, as an opposite, an inverse. Do what I am not.

Because Bonnie takes her teaching seriously, because she listens after class and writes comments on their papers, because she does not recite her poems aloud, the students assume she is a wizened answering machine full of advice and not a woman dependent on the gas in her car not evaporating before her commute.

Bonnie moves toward the door.

The door is often the answer.

Jeffrey follows.

Hands full, she pushes the door with her tits.

She hasn't ever had a mammogram.

She hates these thoughts.

Jeffrey says, "I'm just thinking, and I know this is practical, but…"

Bonnie says, "Practical's good," and thinks of her

tits, dying.

"So how do you make a living with a writing degree?"

Bonnie keeps walking and says, "There are lots of things you can do with a writing degree," and this is true until you acquire the writing degree. "You could teach English. You could be a journalist."

"Teach, like college?"

Bonnie says, "It's tough right now," implying others, not her.

The university barely pays Bonnie so Bonnie is paid in the love of her students but if the students know she is not getting paid then they will not love her anymore because she will be poor and a failure and poor failures do not receive love.

Jeffrey says, "You write, don't you, like do you have a book?"

Bonnie spots her car, parked crooked.

Jeffrey says, "I'd love to read something you wrote. If you have a novel or some stories or poems or whatever, I'd love to take a look. That's obnoxious, huh?"

"No, not at all," Bonnie says.

"First, I hit on you. Then I start bugging you about your book. I'm an idiot."

"It's sweet, really," she says and cannot acknowledge her lack of book.

Jeffrey believes Bonnie to be famous, however small the fame. How weird that the whole world knows nothing about writers and women who teach college.

Jeffrey says, "Professor Colosimo has a couple books."

Bonnie loads her trunk, embarrassed of her dirty and rock-dented car.

Jeffrey says, "Students can buy them in the campus bookstore but I just gave him ten bucks after class. He taught one of his books last semester."

Bonnie stops and focuses and says, "Vincent Colosimo taught his own book?" and she laughs so hard she spits.

Jeffrey pretends not to notice the tiny tear of saliva that flies from Bonnie's mouth and lands on his cheek and sticks and does not roll.

Bonnie says, "I'm sorry. I just spit on you," and she wipes it away like a smudge with her thumb.

"Really?" he says. "I didn't feel it."

"Of course you did."

"Maybe I did."

Bonnie says, "He really taught his own book?"

"Sure," Jeffrey says. "It was just poems."

Bonnie closes the trunk.

Jeffrey says, "I don't get poems."

Bonnie says, "I don't get Vincent fucking Colosimo."

"Me neither."

As Bonnie regrets saying what she said, she says, "Vincent Colosimo is a real fucking retard. I think he's fucking crazy."

"Me too!" Jeffrey says. "You don't teach your own

books. What were we going to say: suckie poems, Dr. Colosimo? That's messed up, right?"

The wind comes across campus, pushing leaves from one set of trees to another. Cigarette butts and empty soda cups from the cafeteria mix in with nature.

Bonnie says, "Just so you know, I never talk shit on other professors."

Jeffrey says, "Why does he write those poems about food?"

"Those aren't real books."

"Dr. Colosimo's books?"

"They're self-published."

"What's self-published? What's the difference?"

Bonnie says, "It's cheating. It's a fake. It means no real press will publish your work because your work fucking sucks."

"He's that bad?" Jeffrey says.

"He's terrible," Bonnie says. "Writing poems about kielbasa is retarded."

"You shouldn't say retarded so much. My brother is retarded."

"I'm sorry," Bonnie says. "I'm a mess."

"I'm kidding. My brother's not retarded."

Jeffrey touches Bonnie on the shoulder, a joke, handing it to her.

She says, "I have a recent gift for missing the obvious."

Jeffrey says, "Why are you rushing away? Don't you stick around and teach another class or have office hours or something?"

"I have to meet a landlord about an apartment."

"I can drive you there."

"Really?" Bonnie says, like she might refuse, but she grabs her purse and is out of the car because she wants to be driven somewhere, needs to be driven, cannot drive herself any more.

Jeffrey says, "I'll go get my truck."

Bonnie says, "I don't have a book. I've never written one."

An empty bag of chips blows past her feet.

Jeffrey says, "That's cool, I get it."

* * *

From the street the apartment appears decent, less run-down than expected, an old duplex split into singles, red brick and green shutters.

Jeffrey waits outside while Bonnie talks to the landlord.

The inside equals the outside, maybe better, newish carpet, a tiny and unexpected washer and dryer in the bathroom. The faucet does not drizzle. Bonnie flushes the toilet and the water rushes away then rises perfectly.

The landlord says, "Good flush, huh?" and laughs. His ears are a jungle of hairs, tiny antennae desperate for sounds. "So what do you do again? You maybe told me on the phone but I hear badly that way. Say it to my right ear," and he turns, more friendly in person, like his apartment.

Bonnie says, "I teach at Allegheny University, the McKeesport campus," thinking one college and one campus sounds better than five colleges and five campuses.

"You teach college?" the landlord says. "That's big time!"

"It's just a branch campus."

"Be proud of yourself. You like the place?"

"The apartment?" Bonnie says. "I love it."

"No security deposit necessary. A lady professor like you can be trusted."

"Thank you," Bonnie says, going into her purse for her checkbook.

"I rented to a guy once. What shit. Never again. No men."

The landlord pulls a pen from his shirt pocket.

Bonnie says, "Thank you," and takes the pen, an old Bic, blue ink, like she used to take notes with back in college, back in high school, when she wanted to hold every word.

* * *

In the truck Bonnie says, "Let's go somewhere and talk," then borrows Jeffrey's cell phone so she can cancel her other classes at other colleges.

Jeffrey drives the truck, an old stick shift, working through the gears.

He says, "So you don't have a book yet?" and Bonnie

appreciates the way he says that, yet, like a book is still a possibility, almost a definite.

* * *

It's noon and Bonnie is already drunk so she orders another beer and a sandwich. The beer is ice cold in an even colder mug, the frost thick enough to wipe with her finger. Because the landlord refused her security deposit, because he trusted her, she has money. She never has money. Money feels so good, better than the beer.

Jeffrey holds up a pack of Marlboro Reds and says, "This is the last bar in the area you can smoke in."

Bonnie bums a cigarette and it tastes terrible until it doesn't and the smoke erases the morning and fills in what was taken and now the afternoon goes as slow and fast as Bonnie wants it to, like she can hold the clock and pull the minutes back. She talks about writing. She talks about books. She picks at her sandwich and drinks another beer. Jeffrey does not know anything about books or writing but he wants to and he wants to learn it from Bonnie. She remembers she knows these things, really knows them, and loves them, and was good at them and can be good at them again.

Jeffrey drinks a glass of water between every beer because he is driving, though he still drinks enough beer to be drunk.

He says, "You're a pretty cool lady. You know that?"

Bonnie picks at a piece of melted cheese hardening

at the edge of her sandwich.

"I do now," she says.

The bartender, who is covered in tattoos, mostly tigers and Japanese letters, who wears a funky black fedora, who looks like one of Bonnie's students, or all of them, says, "The lunch rush is coming. Can I get yinz two anything else before it starts?"

Jeffrey points at Bonnie and says, "You want another beer?"

"I'm fine," Bonnie says, imagining her new apartment, how she will be able to go there on days like this.

Jeffrey finishes his water and rattles the ice cubes in the glass. He picks up his empty beer and shakes the few final drops into his mouth. When the check comes, he grabs it and instantly offers to pay, lifting his hips from the chair and digging for his wallet. He pulls out a credit card, something Bonnie doesn't have anymore.

He says, "Seriously, on me."

Bonnie says, "That's very sweet," and accepts.

YOU NEVER LOVED HIM

Her stepfather was dead and Vanessa had hated him most of her life.

Now she was supposed to attend his funeral.

She stood in front of her closet, an oversized shoebox at the back of her efficiency apartment, and shuffled hangers. The one dress she owned, red with a plunging neckline, was so tight her tits bubbled out. Work and college had changed her shape. She pulled a plastic crate from under her tiny storage area. A black sweater, bulky and conservative, sat on top of the pile. She dug deeper and found black slacks, size eight, not even close. Everything she owned was mauve or baby blue or pink. She once painted her toenails canary yellow. Magenta streaked her blonde hair back in college, the first college, when she was still a teenager and lived on campus and partied and skipped classes and dope-smoked her way to failing out.

The funeral started in two hours. Her head hurt from booze. She shook out six aspirin, tossed them in her mouth, and chugged from a two-liter of Diet Coke.

Her neighbor, Bootsy, whose real name was Debbie Molise, leaned against the closet and sipped coconut water. Bootsy played bass in a cover band with a bunch of other recovering middle-aged alcoholics who'd met at an AA meeting. The band weighed about three hundred pounds, total, and they exercised constantly and smoked cigarettes constantly and chugged Folgers coffee and loved Journey and Bad Company and even worse bands like Toto and Air Supply and Foreigner and Reo Speedwagon.

Bootsy said, "Skip a sandwich and those clothes would fit again."

Vanessa said, "Bootsy, you're only skinny because you live on caffeine and nicotine and run nine miles a day."

"I'm quitting coffee this year and nicotine next year."

"You said that last year."

"It's a process."

Bootsy was okay when she wasn't talking about recovery, when she wasn't preaching some trendy diet or cleanse or whatever self-help book she'd recently read or quoting the Bible or some Sufi poet or recommending a new therapy you could do on yourself. Vanessa struggled with bossy people. She allowed them into her life then dismissed their advice. She wanted not to be friends with Bootsy but she was afraid Bootsy needed a friend.

Bootsy said, "You could jog with me."

Vanessa pulled out a pair of black pants, size twelve, she didn't remember buying. She wrapped the waistband around her neck to see if they still fit.

Bootsy said, "You have beer cans in your trash."

Vanessa said, "That's why I'm hungover."

A little road crew had squeezed into Vanessa's skull

and worked on the front of her brain with hammers, with shovels and picks.

Bootsy said, "Budweiser cans too."

Vanessa said, "Don't remind me."

She hated Bud, how the name was like a guy you'd take fishing, how the aftertaste was beechwood and metal.

Bootsy said, "I count six cans, all pounders."

Vanessa said, "There's a couple more in the fridge if you're taking inventory."

"It's not inventory."

"Then why are you looking in my trash?"

"To see what you've been drinking."

"Coconut water is a sham," Vanessa said. "Everyone knows that."

"Maybe," Bootsy said. "But I can drink coconut water all night and not emerge from a blackout and find myself on the snotty end of some dude's fuck stick."

"That's just gross."

"I know. That's why I don't drink anymore."

"Say nice things. My stepdad just died."

"You said you hated him."

Vanessa said, "Move out of my bathroom doorway so I can try this on," and she took the black slacks and the black sweater and her hangover and pushed Bootsy aside.

* * *

Two night ago, a rare Friday off, Vanessa'd gone to Harry's

Bar, a dive located a couple miles from campus and down the block from the restaurant where she waitressed. She was a regular at Harry's. Daily, sometime two times a day, Vanessa popped in for a drink, for a sandwich, for a quiet spot to study or do homework. She needed the noise of the TV hanging above the bar to clear her head. The lady who owned the place, a retired cop who'd grown tired of having her ass patted by men in uniforms, knew Vanessa's drink, Absolut and Cranberry, and delivered it before Vanessa could find a stool. Vanessa always tipped a dollar, even on a three-dollar drink. Nights, she slid a five in the jukebox and picked songs she knew other customers loved. She chatted up the old people, the people who grew up dancing to Frank Sinatra and Paul Anka and the Lennon Sisters. It was important to Vanessa to be a regular, to have a destination. Her apartment was tiny and cramped and sometimes smelled like ground meat and wet carpet, and Bootsy lived next door, one thin wall away, a new proverb behind old drywall.

Vanessa needed a home.

Because of this, because she believed in bars and her place at the bar, she did not ever meet men or flirt with men or fall in love with the men she talked to at Harry's. She did not make advances or lead guys on. She neither accepted nor made offers for meals or movies or drinks elsewhere. Harry's Bar was a friendly place, a lovely place, and because getting laid was not always friendly and not always lovely, Vanessa did not get laid with men from Harry's Bar.

And then she did.

Davey was twenty-one and looked good in everything, jeans and beat-up khakis and t-shirts and sweaters and jackets he probably bought at the Salvation Army or somewhere expensive and pretended to find at the Salvation Army. He was tall and thin with black hair and a little jazz patch on his chin. He always smelled like cigarettes and soap, not cologne, which Vanessa hated on men, and Davey's hands were rough, something she admired. Rough hands meant work, meant desire. Vanessa thought she would kiss Davey outside the bar, breaking her own rule but in a small way, then she kissed him and moved into the kiss and stayed in the kiss until she stopped kissing him and gave him her address.

She said, "Do you know where that is?"

She said, "You can follow me."

He said, "I will."

It had started like this.

Vanessa had walked in to Harry's on Friday night, she waved at the bartender and the bartender delivered her drink and there, down the bar, on a stool, looking young and beautiful and confident, sat Davey, drinking a bottle of Pabst.

"What are you doing here?" Vanessa said.

"I'm here all the time," Davey said.

"You're not here all the time," Vanessa said. "I'm here all the time."

Davey took a drink of his PBR and said, "Then why haven't I seen you here before?" and raised his eyebrows in a way that was both ridiculous and sexy.

Vanessa and Davey took a couple classes together at college. She liked him but she liked all the young people who were nice to her, all the kids who believed their dreams were a few tuition payments away.

Vanessa pulled up a stool and smelled—despite the beer and cigarettes—cinnamon, not like gum, not like Trident or Dentyne, but like a muffin or fresh bread, like a baker had sprinkled Davey before putting him in the oven.

She said, "You smell like a cookie."

He said, "I work in a bakery."

"You're kidding? Why didn't you ever tell me that?"

"What's up with your poems?" he said. "They're pretty bad."

"I'm not trying to be a poet. I want to be a social worker."

"I want to be a poet."

"I wanted to be a kickboxer," Vanessa said. "I was fourteen."

"Poet is as good as anything else in college," he said.

"Not really," she said, and bought him another Pabst, a beer she despised, and was disappointed in herself for knowing she was going to kiss him outside the bar but excited she could still break her own rules.

* * *

Vanessa had been in college, colleges, sometimes community,

sometimes university, depending on her money and time and interest, for almost twelve years. She'd started out wanting to be a phys-ed teacher because she loved sports, loved playing volleyball, but volleyball at Allegheny East was more like a sorority, more like a party, and the scholarship offers were almost nothing, like a book voucher, so Vanessa eventually quit volleyball to work part-time for UPS because at least UPS offered partial tuition reimbursement. She threw boxes for four years, until her back ached all the time and her knuckles ached all the time and her hands were so dry and cracked Vaseline wouldn't smooth her skin. She quit UPS and upped her student loans.

Now she waited tables and majored in psychology, psychology because last semester an advisor counted her credits and said, "Psychology is the fastest way to graduate." Vanessa knew psychology was useless, like poetry or history or kickboxing, but she talked to a woman in career services and the woman recommended graduate school in social work, a two-year program at the main campus. Vanessa thought she could do that, social work, helping people, maybe teenage girls. She was less sure about main campus, the commute, two more years and another pile of student loans. She drove a 2004 Hyundai. She was almost eighty grand in debt.

Maybe she couldn't help anyone.

* * *

38

Davey wanted to help Vanessa. This was before Harry's Bar and the kiss that turned into sex. He was her workshop partner in Introduction to Poetry. Poetry was the only elective available to Vanessa that wasn't a science. She liked science but science was too hard and nothing was subjective. Vanessa needed her electives to be subjective so she could apologize and beg and flirt to get her grade raised.

Before her poetry class, in the computer lab, Davey looked at Vanessa's poems and cut lines and added words. During class he positioned his tests so Vanessa could see his answers. Vanessa was not above this. She wanted to finish school. A degree was no different than a ticket, only you paid your way out, not in.

* * *

She found a blue knit dress in her sweater drawer. If her mother wouldn't have been hurt, she would have worn pink, pink to celebrate the death of her stepfather, pink shoes and white tights and a pink sweater. She'd be the good witch. Her stepfather was the bad witch. She would have worn a bonnet, something ridiculously pretty, a white one with blue flowers like her stepfather used to make her wear when she was a kid and they went to church three times during Easter week but weren't allowed to have candy baskets or to hunt eggs because eggs and baskets were sacrilegious.

Vanessa rubbed her stomach. She had Budweiser-belly from last night and she couldn't decide if eating something would help or bloat her even more.

Bootsy refilled her coconut water bottle from the tap.

She said, "I'll go with you if you need the support."

"That's sweet," Vanessa said. "But no."

"Embarrassed of me because I'm an alcoholic?"

"Stop. I don't feel like introducing you to people I can't stand. They'll assume we're lesbians, which will be just another thing to deal with."

"Because I play in band and don't wear make-up suddenly I'm your boyfriend?"

"No, because we'd be women alone. People are weird. They think weird things about single women who spend time together."

"I used to be married."

"Exactly."

"Alcohol ruined that."

"Stop," Vanessa said. "No more alcohol talk. My mom's coming to get me soon. She's been covering for me at the viewing, saying I was busy with work and school."

Bootsy said, "Can I meet your mom?"

"No," Vanessa said.

"Because I'll tell her you've been drinking Bud pounders?"

"You're adding to the drama. Please stop. Not everything is about drinking."

"It is for the alcoholic."

"I'm going to ask you to leave if you don't stop."

"I'll stop," Bootsy said.

"Or you can stay and I'll punch you, either way."

"All zipped up," Bootsy said and pretended to lock her lips together.

Vanessa opened the refrigerator. She needed to grocery shop. After a minute she took out a jar of pickles. She thought about her breath and put them back.

Bootsy said, "Pickles are good."

Today was Sunday. Vanessa had never been to a funeral on a Sunday or even known funerals existed on Sundays but her stepfather had been a born-again Christian, that was his thing, talking about god and making people miserable, so maybe he'd planned this, his own special day.

* * *

Vanessa and her stepfather lacked any sort of connection, genetic or otherwise, yet they were both fat with thick waists. It was depressing. He wore his gut like a basket of laundry he never set down. In the summer, shirtless by the pool or cutting the lawn, his flabby chest slopped to points, to furry cones, and his legs were either albino white or sunburned pink, the hair rubbed off his thighs from wearing tweed pants to work for thirty years. Vanessa thought of herself as curvy, and she was, most of the time, except on the weekends when she hammered a large pepperoni from Domino's two nights in a row at one in the morning. Then she felt like a slob.

"This is my weakness," her stepfather once said to Vanessa, pointing to the pie he was inhaling, when she was sixteen and had been caught with beer.

"Pie's not a weakness," she said.

"I'm a glutton," he said. "Maybe you're an alcoholic. We all have struggles." He turned his fork sideways and captured the remaining pie filling. He said, "Food will kill you eventually, I know that, but alcohol brings so much shame. The female doesn't handle alcohol like the male. She doesn't metabolize it the same. My first wife drank in bars with strange men. That's why we are no longer together. I had that one annulled."

He acted like this was sweetness, taking her to a diner before taking her home and grounding her for a month, including phone privileges, but he didn't understand sweetness, not in any real way, just like he didn't understand forgiveness, which was all everyone at church talked about.

He said, "Maybe we'll both do better."

Vanessa pushed her soup away and said, "Just because you're fat doesn't mean I'm an alcoholic. I had three beers over four hours. I was under the limit. I could have legally driven home."

Vanessa leaned to the straw in her Coke and sipped.

Her stepfather tilted his head and squinted one eye.

He said, "I'm sorry, but are you of age? Can you legally have even one beer? No, you cannot. Because you cannot legally have a beer, you are never okay to drink and drive, and you won't be okay to drive after having one beer until you're twenty-one years old. When's that, five more years?" He waited. He counted the years on his fingers. "Sixteen," he said. "Seventeen."

Vanessa wouldn't answer.

"Childish," he said. "You're habitually twelve."

He waved his fork in the air at the waitress who was cleaning the salad bar then he pointed at his plate, meaning more pie.

"You're a man who talks with your fork," Vanessa said. "That's embarrassing."

The pie finally caught him, the ice cream too, and all the burgers and chips and American cheese and chip-chopped ham he ate right from the bag. His heart stopped on the seventh hole at Pine Grove, a public golf course open to anyone with forty bucks who owned a set of clubs. One of her stepfather's friends, Hank Kearns, a recovering pill addict, recently cleaned up, didn't own anything. He'd lost his wife, then his house, then his job, all because of oxycodone. He was only twenty-nine, Vanessa's age. He was new to golf, new to religion. They'd purposely not rented a cart so they could get some exercise. When Vanessa's stepfather's arms went numb, Hank screamed, hoping someone would come. When Vanessa's stepfather fell sideways to the ground, Hank shouted and paced over a man clutching his chest. Then Hank knelt down. He held Vanessa's stepfather's hand. He prayed. Then he ran to the clubhouse and waited for the ambulance, feeling like he'd done this somehow, with his pill addiction and lack of faith.

So said Vanessa's mother on the phone four days ago when she'd called with the news. "Your stepfather passed," she'd said. "It's okay that you never loved him."

"I loved him," Vanessa said, but it was a lie and they both knew it. She'd once told the man, "If god smites anyone, it should be you."

Now, all these years later, she couldn't remember what it meant to be smited or even how to smite someone else, someone like her dead stepfather.

* * *

She held up the blue knit dress and touched her stomach. She wished she could lose some weight, right there, in her middle. After growing up chunky she'd been thin for years without trying then, suddenly, she wasn't. First, she gained ten pounds. Then, in what felt like weeks, she gained twenty more. Her butt filled out nicely, popped even, and her tits looked good in a v-neck t-shirt, even her uniform, but her belly was something else, a weird addition she hadn't planned for. The buttons on her jeans dug into her skin and she couldn't afford new jeans, not a pair with a decent cut, so she mostly wore yoga pants and long shirts.

Bootsy said, "I feel like I should be doing something."

"I have something for you to do," Vanessa said. "Leave."

Bootsy said, "I was hoping to meet your mom."

"Get your own mom," Vanessa said.

She looked at the clock and decided there was plenty of time for a nap.

Bootsy said, "Maybe I could stay? I get lonely."

Vanessa said, "We all do."

She stepped into the bathroom and closed the door and turned on the shower to see if the steam would help with the wrinkles in her blue dress. She had an iron somewhere but couldn't remember if it worked. The hot water in her apartment usually disappeared in minutes and she hated cold showers so she jumped in and scrubbed down until she felt last night's Budweiser disappear in the soap and heat. She dried off quickly with a small hand towel and pulled on some comfies from a basket of clean clothes she'd never folded.

She stepped back into the other room.

Bootsy said, "We're playing tomorrow night down at The Lamp. We're playing with Bon Journey. They play mostly Bon Jovi songs with a few Journey songs mixed in."

"I figured that," Vanessa said.

Bootsy said, "You should come."

"Maybe," Vanessa said, "but I'm so tired right now."

"I get it," Bootsy said. "I'm gone," and finally went home.

* * *

The knocks on the door startled her. Vanessa wore sweatpants, no panties, and a wife-beater. She'd twisted her wet hair into a braid. She'd fallen asleep on her back, on purpose, so she wouldn't get pillow lines on her face. Drool leaked down her cheek.

"Hold on," she said.

She hated when her mom was early and her mom was always early. Vanessa sat up and adjusted her top so her tits looked more even. She stumbled to the door where the knocks sounded like a machine gun on the wooden frame.

"Okay," she said, and when she opened the door, it was Davey, Davey from college, Davey from Harry's Bar, Davey from her bed two nights ago, handsome Davey, all six feet and twenty-one years and the smell of cinnamon and vanilla.

Vanessa stood there.

Davey clutched a huge bouquet of red roses.

"Jesus," she said. "What are those?"

"They're roses," he said. "Thirteen. It's like a baker's dozen."

She said, "That's a lot of flowers."

"One more than a dozen."

"I got that."

"Do you like them?"

She paused and touched her braid. She smoothed her bangs.

She said, "Those aren't necessary."

He said, "Sure they are."

She pulled her wife-beater up so she showed less cleavage.

She said, "I'm serious, those are nice, really nice, but

they aren't necessary, or even realistic." The bouquet was huge. She said, "They're just so fucking red."

He said, "You're not very romantic, huh?" and stepped into her apartment.

He moved like he was in a kids museum, lightly touching things he shouldn't touch.

"I didn't know you were going to show up," she said.

"You should have come to the bar last night."

"Probably not," she said and imagined herself as someone else, the same person, exactly her, but the her she wanted to be, the her she knew she could be.

When Davey had slept here the other night, he slept without waking, without tossing or turning, a young man turned sideways like an enormous fetus, like a human peanut, while the sex had turned Vanessa sober and waked her up so she wanted to do something, something fun, maybe more sex, maybe more talk, maybe check her phone, maybe eat a sandwich or watch a movie on her crappy TV. She got up and had a beer and washed her face and peed and bounced back down on the bed as loud as possible but Davey snored his young-man snores so his nose twitched with air, so his lips fluttered. His mouth putters kept her awake until morning.

"The flowers are sweet," she said. "Really."

"Thanks," Davey said.

"I'm impressed."

"I was trying to impress you."

"You did it."

Vanessa was a good person, not because she was a good person, but because she did good things. It wasn't a thought. It was direction, like going to the bar. She would say nice things to Davey and confuse him with respect and kindness and he would understand he was better than small apartments and waitresses and poor students approaching thirty. In the past Vanessa had complimented men right out of relationships, right out of her life, so she had experience, she could steer Davey back to college and girls his age by assuring him he was exceptional as a student and a baker and a Pabst drinker and even as a lover if he needed to hear that. Almost everything, if done properly, could be done in a decent way, like a cigarette and a blindfold right before the guys with the bad mustaches gunned you down.

Davey said, "I've never bought flowers for anyone."

Vanessa said, "It's like I broke your flower cherry."

"It's exactly like that," he said. "I knew you'd make it special."

"You're a charmer," she said, and meant it on some practical level.

No one, ever, had given her more than a carnation and the last one she received was in seventh grade, dyed purple, from a wimpy boy she couldn't stand who had a crush. It hurt her feelings to think about, being flowerless all these years, even though flowers made her sneeze and she would have rather gone to eat or had a beer.

Davey said, "I wanted to come earlier and bring fresh bread but someone called off and I got stuck working an extra shift." He leaned into her bathroom for a peek then leaned back out. "It looks different in here, now that I'm sober."

He wore a black t-shirt and jeans. Everything was lightly dusted with flour, even his short hair. Vanessa wanted to smell him. She wanted to lean into his chest and inhale then ask him, politely, to leave.

Davey said, "Did you do something in here?"

She said, "It's a one-room apartment. It can't look different."

"There's that picture," he said. "I didn't see that before. Who's the guy?"

The picture was of Vanessa and her mom, at a New Year's Eve party two years ago, but her stepbrother had managed to edge in on their moment.

She said, "That's my stepbrother. He's a douche."

"How come?"

"Just is. Always was. He's eight years older than me and a douche."

Vanessa remembered being ten or eleven and her stepbrother flicking her ear, hard, hard enough to bruise her neck when he missed. He was eighteen, home from college. He'd walk quietly from room to room, a bored giant, no friends around, the summer ahead, and he'd find her alone and flick, fast, his finger popping against her cartilage. If she heard him coming, which she seldom did because he was such a good sneak, she'd dive to the floor and roll like she was on fire and cover her head with pillows. She hated his touch, his voice, to be near him. Later, when she'd made it through puberty, he tried to feel her tit. She was on the couch, watching TV, lazy, closing her eyes to sleep then glancing at whatever was on. When she realized what he was doing, she grabbed his hand, hard, like she could break his fingers, and said, "Why are you trying to touch my tit?" and he said, "I'm not." She said, "You are." She bent his hand so his wrist turned, so she held the power, but she still felt his prints on her breast, his mark. She said, "I caught you." She said, "I caught you touching my tit," and released his hand and stood so she could run if she needed too. She said, "You're gross." He smiled like the skin on his face had been pulled too tight and said, "I wasn't touching your tit."

He said, "I was checking for lumps."

Now Vanessa turned to Davey and said, "I'm kind of in a hurry."

Davey said, "Did you skip the bar last night to avoid me?"

She said, "No." She said, "Of course I did."

"Why?"

Vanessa thought about her stepbrother and how weak he was, what a coward he was, how lucky she had been, because if he would have been strong, he would have hurt her, she was sure of it, and she was sure her stepfather would have turned it to ice cream and talk.

Davey said, "I was thinking that maybe you not being into flowers would somehow make you more impressed that I brought flowers. I might have messed up somewhere."

Vanessa said, "I'm into flowers," thinking maybe she was.

She looked at her blue dress folded neatly on the bed. She wanted to tell her mom, whom she loved, her mom who had done everything to get Vanessa a home in the suburbs away from her real father who wanted to drive race cars and sleep with biker chicks, her real father who Vanessa never knew, Vanessa thought she would say, "Mom, I can't go to the funeral, I'm sorry." She'd say, "It's not that I didn't love him but that I hated him," and she'd say, "I hated him and god and his fucking kids." She'd say, "They wanted to kill me, all of those creeps," even if they didn't want to kill her, even if she only remembered it that way sometimes, times like now, her childhood shaped like an axe swinging for her skull.

Vanessa looked at Davey and said, "I like you. You're great. I really appreciate you helping me in poetry class. I bet all the girls on campus really dig you and they should. But you're too young for me."

Davey said, "I don't *help* you in poetry class. I do your work, all of it."

Vanessa said, "Fine, you let me cheat off you. I'm a cheater. Thank you."

"I'm not too young."

"You think you're not too young."

"I'm the same as you."

Davey walked over to Vanessa's desk, her only piece of furniture that wasn't a bed or dresser or kitchen cabinet. He pulled out the chair but didn't sit down.

She said, "Davey, thank you for the flowers. I really do appreciate them."

He said, "You're welcome. I probably should have brought you a carton of cigarettes or a bottle of beer."

She said, "I have to get dressed for a funeral."

He stacked her papers, moved her textbooks, and sat down on the desk.

He said, "You want me to come? I could come. Both my parents are dead. I know about funerals. I have other clothes."

She said, "Thank you but no."

He said, "I own a house. It's not big. It needs a new furnace. When my parents died, there was insurance money. I bought a house. My sister spent her share on shoes. She's really smart but she does stupid shit. She has ten thousand pairs of shoes and she lives with a guy who won't let her have any friends. He's a state cop in Philly."

Vanessa knew she would get through this day, because she got through every day, and then it would be better, but Davey, but the funeral, but her mom.

She said, "Davey, I want to help you. But, honestly, what can I do for you?"

He said, "I don't want help." He said, "I really like you. I have a fulltime job and I own a house and I go to school. No offense, but you're a terrible student and your apartment sucks. You should let me come to the funeral. I'll beat up your stepbrother."

Vanessa said, "You don't even know who died."

"Your stepdad," he said. "How drunk were you when we fucked?"

"Oh god," she said. "You're making this weird. You were such a nice fuzzy memory until you showed up at my door."

Davey climbed off the desk and walked to her cabinet, a tiny wooden box with a scuffed metal handle, in the corner of her apartment that was supposed to be a kitchen.

He opened the door and said, "I know you don't have a vase but I thought you'd have a wine bottle or something."

Vanessa looked at the roses and said, "I have a vase," because she wanted to be the kind of person who had vases, who knew flowers were always on the way.

Davey said, "Do you want me to eat your pussy again?"

She said, "No," but didn't remember the first time.

Then she sort of remembered it in a good way.

Davey said, "I was joking."

He said, "Let's chat."

They passed some time then Vanessa agreed to see Davey again, maybe not a date, something that official, but for a drink. He could stop over. She would meet him at the bar. They would get something to eat between classes, like a beer. Time might turn her into a liar but she mostly believed what she said and he needed to leave and she needed to concentrate on the funeral. Her mom, always early, was almost late.

Davey said, "I haven't had a lot of girlfriends."

Vanessa said, "That's because you're twenty-one."

Davey said, "You didn't let me finish. I was going to say I haven't had a lot of girlfriends because I don't get along with girls my age."

"Maybe you should try," Vanessa said.

"Yeah," Davey said, smiling, rubbing his hairy bottom lip. "When you were twenty-one, did you date any bakers with dead parents who were studying poetry?"

Vanessa moved into the bathroom with her blue dress. She came back for the roses and put them in the shower. She'd have to skip panties because she didn't feel like she could pull out a clean pair in front of Davey even though he'd seen her naked, even though she'd lifted her hips so he could get her clothes off.

She closed the door but not the whole way.

She said, "A baker poet would have been great when I was twenty-one. I was dating cokehead lawyers who thought they were gods."

Davey said, "Could I come in there? I'll sit on the toilet and we can talk."

Vanessa was naked. She needed tights. If she went digging for tights, she might as well dig out some clean underwear.

She peeked from the bathroom door and said, "Davey, I'll see you soon."

He said, "Do you know what you're going to say yet?"

She sighed and said, "I said yes. I said we'll see each other again."

"Not me," he said. "At the funeral."

He'd moved to her bed. He stretched out. His shoes were off and the bottoms of his white socks were dirty brown.

Vanessa said, "I'm going to say nothing at the funeral. He was my stepfather. I hated him. Why would I have to say something?"

"That's what people expect."

"What people?"

"The ones who will want you to speak."

"No, they won't. I haven't said ten words to the guy in years."

"They'll want you to speak," he said. "A poem or something."

She considered this and it sounded awful enough to be true. Fake people, even in death, required fakery, theatrics. Maybe she'd be expected to cry. Maybe she'd be expected to read something from the Bible or hand out scrolls of paper with inspirational messages or give flowers to the pallbearers. People loved to tell lies when they should be telling the truth. Vanessa wanted so much to be true. She wanted to picket her stepfather's funeral, to carry a sign around the church. She wanted to step naked from the bathroom and walk to Davey and lay with him on the bed and take his clothes off and do what they'd done on Friday night, only sober, only better.

She wanted so many things, that's why she had so little, she knew it.

She closed the bathroom door and put the lid down on the toilet and sat and repeated, "Do not cry," until she stopped crying.

Davey said, "Are you crying in there?"

Vanessa said, "Fuck off."

"I could write you something," Davey said.

"You can leave, Davey," Vanessa said, sticking her face out the door. "Like right now, like I asked you to do five minutes ago."

"Could I kiss you first?" he said.

She pulled her face back to look in the mirror. The light shined bright and showed lines when she squinted but so what. It was a beautiful face if you really considered it, if you were twenty-one and a baker and a poet and liked this kind of face, how it was round but maybe not fat, how the skin was clear, and if you focused on the face, Vanessa's face, which she scrubbed and moisturized every night no matter how tired or drunk she was, if you moved close to her face, you would see the beauty, and only the beauty, instead of the rest of her world.

She opened the door.

"The sick thing here is that I want you to kiss me," she said as she came from the bathroom without even her towel.

* * *

Vanessa's mom, Angeline, pronounced lean, not line (so she always said), stunned in a new black dress, black hose with little paisley designs, and black high heels. She was only forty-seven. People guessed thirty-five. The charmers said thirty. She'd started exercising when she'd turned forty and the years had rolled back. Her hair was newly dyed, a blackish blue that somehow looked natural. A gray streak cut through her bangs but she wanted it that way.

Vanessa modeled her own dress and felt like a schlub.

Angeline said, "Blue is an excellent color for your skin tones. You look gorgeous. I wasn't even hoping for black."

Vanessa said, "I don't own any black."

"I was afraid you were going to wear yellow."

"I don't have a fancy purse."

Angeline said, "Oh, who cares?" and dismissed the whole thing.

Vanessa picked up her ID and some money she always kept clipped together. Her mom sat on the bed. She stretched out her legs and smoothed her skirt. Her legs were long and thin and still sexy. Dancer's legs.

Vanessa said, "We're going to be late."

Her mom said, "We have time."

Vanessa stopped by the door and said, "Are you okay?"

She meant it.

Vanessa wanted to know what happened inside her mother, to her mother's heart, what she'd had to do and what she'd done and what had been done to her all week since the moment a strange man had called and said her husband had dropped dead on a golf course. Vanessa wanted to know it all but Angeline kept secrets, was a secret, a whole bank of things she'd never say. Angeline had always made Vanessa feel loved and Vanessa had always trusted Angeline with everything, even the worst, but how Angeline felt was a mystery, like some scientific fact Vanessa had learned in school but didn't know, not really. Angeline had married a dirt track racer and he'd gotten her pregnant then left her then she'd married a putz. Vanessa endlessly wondered about her dad, not as her dad but as the man her mom had loved so seriously she'd been willing to accept another man she could never love.

Vanessa said, "I know you don't like to talk about this but can we talk about this? Tell me if you're okay. Please. I'm your daughter."

Angeline picked a piece of lint from her skirt and sighed. Vanessa walked to the bed and sat down. She pictured Davey there, his face above hers.

"Tell me you're okay," Vanessa said to her mom.

"I'm not okay," Angeline said.

Vanessa said, "I'm sorry I didn't come to the funeral home."

"Who cares about that, it was boring."

"I have all kinds of excuses but I could have come."

Angeline said, "It was nothing at all, really."

She reached out and took Vanessa's hand. Vanessa moved closer. Angeline was not crying. She was not, as far as Vanessa could tell, sad.

Angeline said, "My husband just died. I've been three nights at the funeral home, talking to his friends, and now we're going to do the same thing again, and then drop him in a hole at the cemetery. I'll toss some dirt on his coffin in a dramatic gesture. That's it, I guess. I'm not okay. I'm something else. I don't know the word for it yet."

Vanessa glanced up at her mom and said, "You look okay."

Angeline said, "I don't know. Maybe I feel okay."

Vanessa knew Angeline did not love her husband, Vanessa's stepfather, and had never loved him and that she'd married for safety, for the chance to get Vanessa away from Wilkinsburg where their apartment had been robbed three times in two years, where the windshield on Angeline's car had been kicked in and the side mirrors had been kicked off and the locks picked and broken and all four tires slashed on two separate occasions. Husbands were tickets too, like college degrees, only husbands paid out in cars and clothes and good schools and houses in safe neighborhoods. Vanessa knew that her mother would never admit this, or that she would say, as she had before, "There are all kinds of love," but love was love, not a paycheck or payout or a payday. Or her mom was right.

Her mom was probably right.

Vanessa said the only kind thing she could think to say, "You were a good wife."

Angeline picked up a pillow and covered her lap. She said, "You and I both know I was better than that."

* * *

Angeline wanted a beer. She was not a drinker. Her husband didn't believe in drinking so booze was never around. Vanessa cracked the tops of the two cans of Bud left in the fridge and handed one to her mom.

Angeline said, "People still drink Bud?"

Vanessa said, "Unfortunately, yes."

"Bud's good, isn't it?"

"Bud is not good anymore."

"Well, what's good?" Angeline said, delicately sipping from the can.

Vanessa said, "I don't know, anything but Bud, maybe East End or Full Pint. People drink microbrews now. A good beer costs six bucks in a dive bar."

Angeline said, "Don't hate me."

They cuddled on the bed, in their funeral clothes, under the covers. It was warm there, leg against leg. Vanessa's basement apartment, even during summer, was cool and damp. She sipped at the Bud, which tasted better when you used it to help with something, something like a hangover or a funeral.

Vanessa said, "How could I ever hate you?"

Angeline drank off her beer. She swallowed and let out a delicate burp.

She said, "Randy wants you to say something."

Randy was Vanessa's stepbrother.

"At the funeral?"

"Yes, at the funeral. Where else would you say something? Come on, Vanessa, sweetie, you're in college. Use your head."

"But why?"

"Because they're church people. It's what they do. Image is everything. You're the loving stepdaughter."

This is where Vanessa should have used the excuse she'd planned since talking with Davey. It went: no and I can't and I won't, not now, that's over, fuck them, the creepers, fatty and the molester, no fucking way, I'm fucking out.

But, instead, she said, "Ah Mom, please," and sounded childish.

Angeline said, "There's money in it."

Vanessa said, "You want to pay me? That's insulting."

Angeline said, "No one is insulting you." She said, "It's all insulting, honey."

Vanessa looked at her mom, the gray streak falling across her blue eyes, and said, "I'd do anything for you," which was not true but felt right to say.

"Not money for reading something. Pay attention." Angeline snapped two times at Vanessa, close enough to make her blink. Angeline said, "Come back to me." She said, "You're in the will. It's not a lot, but it's money you can use. He didn't think you were college material but if you graduated, he wanted you to have something, like a reward."

Vanessa said, "I don't want his money."

Angeline scooted up on their pile of pillows and said, "Are you kidding me?"

"I am not kidding."

"You are kidding."

"Why am I kidding?"

Angeline pressed a pillow to her face and sighed.

Then, with the pillow still over her face, she screamed. It was more painful than Vanessa had ever seen her mom.

Angeline took down the pillow.

She breathed deeply.

She said, "Okay, you're not kidding."

Vanessa thought of her mom, her beautiful young mother, her beautiful middle-aged mother, her beautiful mother approaching fifty, in bed all those years with someone she didn't love, with someone she may have despised. Vanessa scooted down on the pile of pillows. She wanted the money, maybe all of it, all but her mother's share.

Angeline said, "Randy is co-executor. That means he's half in charge. I don't want to fight him on anything. If you're not going to say something nice, it'd be better if you didn't come. I'll make up an excuse."

Vanessa said, "No, I'll say something."

"You don't have to."

"What will I say?"

"If you really want to do it, you'll think of something. Or don't, sweetie, that's okay too. I could have handled this better. I'm not at my best right now."

Vanessa looked at the ceiling and imagined her stepfather in the plaster, a swirl of lines making a cloud, a fat golfer with a dog's face. She started to write the speech in her head: my stepfather hated me, I hated him back, that's how we managed, I'm glad he's dead, he's pissed I'm still alive, let's sing a Christian song, he liked those. She squinted and changed the lines of plaster so her stepfather was a pig with a human pig face. She made him a monster, a character from Maurice Sendak. She tried to remember something positive. He was great with hamburgers and the grill. My stepfather could flip a burger over fire, folks. He loved tongs.

Angeline said, "It will be fine."

Vanessa said, "Randy touched my tit when I was like fourteen."

Angeline pulled off the covers and let her legs fall to the floor. She stood up and found her purse. She took out an old tissue and blew her nose.

She said, "I know. He told. He told his father. He didn't mean it, honey. He got confused. It was confusing for everyone. I'm not making excuses for him. It was a terrible thing to do and he was old enough to know better. We made him promise it would never happen again and it didn't." She paused then asked, "Correct?"

Vanessa said, "Correct."

She felt embarrassed for even remembering the

moment, let alone making it something else, a rape, a near rape, almost incest, step-incest.

Angeline said, "Take your own car and follow me to the funeral then you can scooch away before we get to the cemetery."

Vanessa said, "I'll stay with you."

Angeline smiled and said, "Don't worry, I'll cover."

Vanessa said, "My neighbor is a recovering alcoholic."

Angeline said, "They're as crazy as the Christians sometimes."

She said, "At least it's sunny," and walked out the door.

* * *

Outside, Davey sat in his old Volkswagen Jetta, window down, a yellow tablet on the steering wheel and a pen in his hand. He waved at Vanessa. The sun was bright and Vanessa shielded her eyes. She'd always wanted expensive sunglasses.

Angeline said, "Who's that boy? He's cute."

Vanessa said, "That boy is Davey," and walked towards his car.

The engine to the Jetta quietly hummed.

Vanessa didn't know if Davey had been waiting or if he'd left and come back.

She said, "Hey."

Davey said, "Your mom's hot."

"I know my mom's hot. I'll tell her you think so."

"I wrote you something. I didn't know your stepfather, so I kept it general, but I think it will work. It's sort of a bad poem-type thing. So your specialty."

He extended the tablet through the open window and Vanessa took it.

She said, "Not all my poems are bad."

Davey said, "No, they really are."

She said, "You can be a cunt."

He said, "Maybe. But I won't ask to kiss you in front of your mom."

Davey's dark square printed letters marched across the yellow paper, a hand-drawn arrow pointing to more words on the next page. A few lines had been scratched out. Mostly, it was clean. Vanessa leaned down towards his face and, in the shade of his car, she saw the tiny lines around his eyes, the patch of hair below his lip, a few gray hairs mixed in with the brown.

"Do you like it?" he said.

"It's okay," she said, and reached for his mouth with hers.

NOT LIKE THE OTHER PEOPLE
IN THE CAR

"Dude, you're a pussy," she said.

Wayne kept making pizza boxes. He hated working with Cara. She ate more pepperoni than she sliced and she always called him names, some variation on vagina. They were the same age and took classes together at the same shitty college but Cara lived on campus and Wayne commuted. Cara liked to smoke dope and steal boyfriends and brag about both. She liked to tan. She liked to shop at the mall. Even in winter she wore tight t-shirts and short-shorts to work. She never wore a bra. She needed a bra. When she bent to the cans of sauce in the stockroom, her ass crack slid out. When she stood, she only hiked up one side of her shorts or yoga pants so a tanned ass cheek and her bunched up underwear always stayed visible. Sometimes she'd say to Wayne, "Quit looking at my ass, you fucking fruitcake."

Wayne stopped folding cardboard and said, "Why am I a pussy?"

"Because you *are* a pussy," Cara said. "There doesn't have to be a reason for a dude like you to be a pussy. You just are. It's a Zen thing."

Wayne walked to the register and swapped out his

twenties for smaller bills to make change on his next round of deliveries. The guy out front, the owner, kept on, tossing dough, stocking the cooler. The owner refused all the online bullshit—no overpriced delivery stuff, no apps, no nothing. Wayne walked back to the oven. He knew not to engage Cara because anything would allow her to twist her mind to some new attack.

Then, out of dignity, he said, "What do you know about Zen?"

She said, "Enough."

"What makes you such an expert?"

"I didn't say I was an expert."

"Exactly," Wayne said.

Wayne had read a book on Buddhism for a class. He couldn't remember if he'd finished it. He'd tried to read the Koran but ended up skimming. He wanted to know things but it was hard to know things and it took work and time without pay, like the pizza shop but the opposite.

Cara said, "I know you're a pussy, that's what I know about Zen."

Wayne said, "Why are you so awful?"

Cara said, "Don't be such a cunt," and pressed her middle finger to her nose.

Maybe Wayne was a pussy.

Delivering pizzas made him feel like one.

He ducked eye contact and looked over people's shoulders when they answered their doors. He counted back their change and never waited for a tip because it embarrassed him, even though he needed tips, even though he made minimum wage, even though most people said, "Hey," and called him back and handed him a buck or two or sometimes a five.

Now he pulled up at an apartment complex, six scrubby units. He climbed out and rang the front door. A woman buzzed and asked who was there.

Wayne said, "Pizza."

She said, "Leave it."

She had an Ethel Merman voice, a black-and-white movie voice.

Wayne said, "I can't leave it."

She said, "Sure you can. I paid on a card."

"You have to sign the slip."

"Shit."

"Sorry," Wayne said.

She came down in fuzzy pink sweatpants and a man's t-shirt. No make-up. Knotty blonde hair. She was skinny as a methhead and smoking a menthol cigarette.

She said, "I guess someone expects a tip."

Wayne said, "I'm fine," his eyes going down.

"Kidding," she said and handed Wayne the signed receipt and two dollars.

Wayne said, "Thanks." He said, "You should be in pictures."

She said, "Now you're just being an asshole."

Wayne said, "I didn't mean to," and walked off.

He found his car and put the tip in an envelope.

He started the car and revved the engine.

Wayne drove a Ford Focus. He'd bought the car for eight hundred dollars, its exact Blue Book value, from his dad. The car needed a new battery. On cold mornings Wayne coasted downhill and popped the clutch. It was embarrassing, like living at home after high school, like buying a car when you wanted to buy a motorcycle when your dad said, "Nothing on two wheels." Then his dad said, "Not in my house," which is what he'd been saying since Wayne was five. "Piss the bed? Not in my house."

Wayne could have bought a Honda 750 street bike with a one-year warranty and saved fifty dollars a week in gas.

* * *

It was Saturday night. All of Wayne's friends were away at college, living in dorm rooms or apartments, drinking canned beer and hanging out with girls who wanted to be filmed while they fingered themselves. Wayne had never been on a real college campus, one where students didn't have to find parking spots. He'd never wanted that but he sort of did.

He pulled up at a stoplight by Luigi's Italian Restaurant and waited for the green arrow. A couple more deliveries and he'd circle back. He had sixty bucks in tips, decent money, except for tuition, except for car repairs.

Wayne checked his cell for texts. There was one from Cara. It said: pussyfuck. None of his old pals from high school kept in touch. They were busy, he guessed. It was tough getting laid and doing beer bongs like in the movies.

He texted Cara back: please stop.

Tomorrow, there'd be church.

That was the rule: you live at home, you go to church.

His mother loved church but it made her nervous.

Wayne loved his mother but she made him nervous.

She tweaked and flashed. She had habits requiring repetition. To be near her when she started pacing was to watch carpet turn to lint. She washed her face until the skin around her nose cracked. On Sundays she attended church twice. On Wednesdays she attended once. Before the services she palmed a quarter in each hand while walking the house in direct lines, tracing the outskirts of rooms, as his father slowly pulled on a bad tie. His dad hated ties. He had enormous hands and drove a dump truck. He hadn't hit Wayne since the summer after high school. There had been blood on Wayne's face and on his father's shirt and Wayne had purposefully placed his face against the living room wall to make a mark.

Wayne loved his mom, sort of.

* * *

A man in a cowboy hat said, "This cowboy hat don't make me a badass if that's what you're thinking," and handed Wade a stack of newly-straightened ones to pay for his pizza.

Wayne said, "Thanks," and meant it.

A cowboy hat was a hard sell.

Wayne stopped on a backroad to arrange his money bag. The moon shone so bright, Wayne didn't need to use the inside light of the car.

He stopped counting and looked to space, to the moon and stars.

He hadn't done that in years.

The next light turned yellow and Wayne braked for it. An SUV pulled up, music blaring. The bass rocked Wayne's car. He hoped it was rich girls who wanted to get his attention but it sounded like dudes, like guys in hoodies and fake gold chains. It sounded like guns. Wayne liked acoustic guitars. He liked music that no one else listened to. He liked Benny Calhoun. He liked the song "I Used To Paint Houses Before I Tended Bar" and he knew all the words, even the different choruses.

The light turned and he stepped on the gas.

Wayne's Ford didn't have a stereo—no CD player, no radio, nothing. No bluetooth. During the week he wore headphones and jammed his iPod but it was the weekend and the cops were out looking for drunk drivers and Wayne had convinced himself he could be pulled over and arrested for wearing headphones. This was the kind of paranoid feeling you got from living at home with religious parents. Wayne hadn't smoked weed in two years. He used to love smoking weed. Cara smoked weed while she worked. She flicked ashes on the pizzas. She said, "The only people who don't smoke weed are twats."

Wayne delivered two more pizzas. He got a single and a five. A five was great. Once a month some drunk would throw a twenty in a big-shot way but a five was still the goal.

He drove back to Luigi's, blowing through yellow lights. He parked in the handicapped space and hustled inside.

Mark, who owned Luigi's, who was not Italian, who was probably Irish or English or originally from Ohio, said, "Please don't park in the fucking handicap space. Park in front of the building like you're not retarded. The front's closer and it's being respectful." Mark wore wife-beater tank tops and flowered shorts. Sometimes he wore dress shoes without socks.

Wayne said, "How many orders?"

Mark said, "It's slowing down. It'll pick up again in an hour. Any hot bitches?"

Wayne said, "Not yet."

Cara yelled from the back, "Any hot dudes?"

Wayne ignored her.

Mark said, "Your fucking mom called. Twice. She's a kooky bitch."

"Sorry about that," Wayne said.

Mark said, "It's not your fault your parents are fucking kooks. Trust me. My mom is probably up in heaven, making up a reason to hit me with a fucking spoon." He said, "Seriously, no hot bitches?"

Wayne said, "I'll report back when I see anything."

Mark was always concerned with the quality of

female that his pizzas reached. Occasionally, if the lady placing the order sounded hot, he would make the delivery himself. Wayne didn't mind this. Mark still gave him the tip and it was a nice break to be in the store, drinking free Mountain Dews, up front and away from Cara.

Mark said, "I need ten minutes. Can you do the dough? If I leave it, it gets fucking hard and won't toss."

Mark was a cokehead. A guy in Wayne's psych class sold Mark the blow. Wayne tried to pretend it wasn't a big deal. He figured a buzz was a buzz, drugs were drugs, unless coke was crazy like in the movies, guys shooting guns, women running around topless. Wayne wanted to try it, just a line or two or however many it took to get high, but he always lacked the money and Mark never did it in front of him anyway.

One time Cara said, "He's not gonna let you do any of his blow if you keep acting like a bitch," then she flicked her joint over a pizza before she ovened it.

Now Wayne walked over and reached for the bowl of dough.

Mark said, "Seriously. It's the restaurant business. Wash your fucking hands."

Mark pulled up his flowered shorts and tucked in his wife-beater. Last month he turned forty but he looked thirty, maybe thirty-two or thirty-three, like cocaine was packed with vitamins. He had a goatee but he hated to shave so most days it blurred into his hairy face.

Wayne said, "I washed my hands."

Mark said, "Like an hour ago. You're gonna give everyone VD or some shit."

* * *

Wayne loaded up his deliveries. One order, six large pizzas, he hoped would land him a monster tip. He hoped the customer would be drunk and high, a woman with huge tits. He had these fantasies. There'd be a silk robe and a lot of dirty talk. He'd get blown like in a porno. He'd eat pussy and be an expert. He'd tell Mark and Mark would promote him to assistant manager. They'd do a bunch of blow to celebrate.

Mark said, "You ever think about fucking Cara?"

Wayne said, "No."

Mark nodded and said, "I wish I wouldn't have hired her."

Wayne said, "Yeah, she's pretty awful," and headed out.

It was eleven o'clock, still early. When the bars closed, the drunks got hungry and Luigi's stayed open. Tomorrow, before church, Wayne would be too tired to shower and he'd stink like sauce, like pizza grease and oregano. He'd fall asleep and his mom would pull his arm hair and his dad, after the service, would say, "Goddamn it, Wayne."

* * *

He turned into The Village, a sprawling apartment complex

in Irwin with dozens of units, all dirty brick with warped siding. Most of the renters got government money. Wayne found 4D and rang the bell. The front door, along one edge, had been covered in NASCAR stickers, mostly drivers' numbers, a few emblems for different brands of oil. A cartoon character pissed on Richard Petty's head. Wayne hated racing.

An old man in a bathrobe opened the door. Wiry gray hairs grew out from his chest like they were being pulled by magnets. His ears were too big. The body of the robe was red but the sleeves were green and a green belt looped around the waist and finished in a sloppy bow like a Christmas decoration.

Wayne said, "Fifteen…" and pulled the receipt closer to make the numbers.

Before he could name the change, the man said, "Here," and handed over a twenty and took the pizza box.

Wayne started for his wad of singles.

The man waved him off.

Wayne said, "Are you sure?"

He said, "Keep it. I'm drunk."

The next delivery was a stiff. A young fat guy—shirtless, gym shorts, Pirates cap turned backwards—paid with a wad of singles and a jar of change, down to the exact penny.

The dude said, "I'll get you next time, bro."

Wayne didn't mind being stiffed except he did, except he knew. He sometimes stood in front of a customer with green tattoos and moles growing from odd places and thought he should be the one giving the tip.

The world was a crooked planet.

Wayne hated that.

The last house was a mansion, two stories of brown brick and stone, probably four or five bedrooms and three or four bathrooms. Lights on motion detectors clicked on as Wayne rolled up. The porch wrapped around to the backyard. He counted nine windows.

From the sideyard a kid on a bicycle, maybe ten or eleven or twelve years old, raced through the grass then skidded across the driveway towards Wayne's car. The kid stopped by rocking forward on his front wheel. Then he leaned back and extended his palms. Wayne popped the Focus in park and rolled down his window.

The kid, who was shirtless, who had skinny-kid muscles, who was shoeless and dressed in cut-off sweatpants, said, "You delivering here?"

Wayne said, "Yeah."

"That house is packed with hot bitches."

"Okay?"

The kid said, "Gimme five bucks."

"For what?"

"For I just gave you a hot tip."

"I was already here. I was pulling up."

"For I prepped you. Now you know hot bitches are inside."

Wayne, being a sport, said, "I'll give you a dollar."

"Deal," the kid said and reached into the window and took the buck.

"Thanks for the info."

"Hot bitches for life," the kid said, and pedaled away.

Wayne parked and climbed out, carrying a huge stack of pizzas. He knew this plan, these people. They answered the door fully dressed, never in sweats or pajamas or a bathrobe, and tipped obnoxiously well on their credit cards. Inside, their walls were painted deep colors and family pictures taken in professional studios hung at perfect angles. Their carpet always felt like a mattress, smooshie and nice.

He stepped onto the porch and rang the bell. The door opened. Wayne looked away like always, hot bitches or not. He reached for the receipt, which had been taped to the top box, and squinted to see the total. He needed glasses. He couldn't afford glasses.

He said, "Seventy-six dollars even."

Six pizzas were a lot to hold with one hand. You had to use your chin.

"One second, I'm sorry," she said, and launched a hand into her purse like the purse was bottomless. "I have cash in here somewhere."

She was hot with straight brown hair and tan skin, maybe from the sun or because she was Italian or Greek or half-Indian, and she wore a loose t-shirt which showed her chest, not her tits, but her chest, a whole infield of beautiful brown skin which was somehow sexier than tits, than boobs falling out.

Wayne's fantasies were fantasies, not goals, not dreams. He knew he wasn't the kind of pizza guy who could get laid on deliveries, who could get a date, who could get a phone number, who could start a genuine conversation with a hungry stranger who was too busy or tired to cook. He was happy to steal glances from customers who didn't look like ogres and take their beauty and make it last.

The woman said, "Sorry," and kept rooting in her purse.

Wayne said, "Take your time," and leaned around the stack of boxes to take another look and he recognized the woman, a girl really, this person his age, and her voice echoed back to high school. Her name was Megan and she'd been his lab partner.

Wayne thought: oh shit.

It wasn't panic but sadness.

A few months ago Wayne had delivered a pizza to an auto-body shop. The parking lot mixed gravel and mud with giant potholes.

The outside light barely lit anything.

Inside, he recognized a couple guys from high school, guys who took shop classes and still failed out, dudes who punched random people in the arms until bruises appeared then burned each other with cigarettes for fun. Wayne hadn't seen them in two years or more and he hoped they had forgotten him but they knew. Their greasy faces lit up with recognition.

One said, "You're the fucking science geek. I

remember your science," and the other said, "How's all that science working out for you?"

They were drunk, drinking canned beer.

They wore boots and coveralls and stood around a junky car on blocks.

Wayne handed over the pizza.

They set the box on the hood of the car.

No one offered to pay.

Wayne waited.

One opened the box and shone a work light on the pizza. The other guy pulled out a slice, tugging but not losing the cheese, a wrench dangling from his other hand. He bit the pizza with meanness.

Wayne backed out of the garage, happy there were no more words, happy there were no punches in the arm or cigarette burns.

* * *

Now, Wayne stood in front of Megan.

He had been afraid to approach her before, on the level playing field of high school, and now he wished she was a mechanic, a man who might treat his arm like an ashtray. Getting your ass kicked was nothing compared to getting humiliated by anonymity. Wayne learned that from his dad who delivered both.

Megan said, "Hey."

Wayne, pretending she was not about to recognize

him, said, "Take your time."

She said, "No, seriously—hey."

At least he didn't wear a uniform.

At least Mark, the cokehead who ran Luigi's, was a good guy who didn't expect his employees to wear name tags and polo shirts that looked like the Italian flag.

Megan extended the money and said, "I know you."

Wayne said, "Yeah, I remember you. Rita, from Bio, right?"

Megan said, "Megan from Chemistry."

Wayne said, "Right, definitely," and he knew he sounded like a fake. He'd called her Rita because he never got laid and wanted to.

She said, "I always tell that joke you told me."

Wayne moved his shoulders like he couldn't remember the joke but he remembered the joke and where he'd told it and how stoned he was and how he'd hoped to be charming, hoped to get a date with Megan, who was wonderful.

She said, "You know—I hope to die in my sleep, quiet and peaceful like my grandfather, and not screaming like the other people in the car."

Wayne said, "That's a good one."

Megan was shoeless, her toenails painted black, a couple toes covered in jewelry. Wayne wanted to suck them, her bejeweled toes, but not creepy, just sincere. No wonder he pretended to lose her name. Her feet were better looking than his face.

He said, "You have jewelry on your toes."

She said, "They're toe rings."

She wiggled her toes.

Wayne said, "I didn't know you could do that."

Inside, the house was huge but empty. The walls were bare, painted white or still primered. The floors were hardwood, not covered with carpet or rugs. Past the barren living room and into the dining room, the usual spot for a table had never been filled. The whole house was like a place that needed to become a place.

Wayne said, "Did you get robbed?"

Megan said, "It's Sherrie Gifford's house. Do you remember her? She has blond hair. Used to date Mark Stinson. Her gigantic boobs are sort of her calling card."

He set the boxes on the floor and stood up with burning hands.

"I don't think I remember her," Wayne said, and his dick chubbed over the way she mentioned boobs, how casual. He adjusted his shirt so it covered his crotch.

What he wanted to say was: I'm not a loser, I do more than deliver pizzas, I hope to be a pharmacist or an engineer or a scientist, I'm making all As, I used to love you in high school, I still do, please.

What he said was, "Are you home for the weekend?"

She said, "Just home-home. I still live with my mom."

"Me too," he said and shrugged like they'd both crawled from the same dismal spot, a hole crowded with parents. "With my mom and dad both."

"That's cool."

"Not really. Where do you go to school?"

He hoped she attended the community college. The community college was the only place worse than a branch campus, especially Allegheny East where the VP had recently knocked up a student and the VP's assistant, who all the students said the VP banged, had been arrested for drunk driving. If Wayne could be better than Megan in some small way, he hoped she could consider him as something else.

She said, "I'm still in high school, silly."

"I thought you were in my grade."

"I was in all AP classes, a sophomore."

"Two years behind me?"

She put her hand on him and shoved, smiling.

Wayne stumbled back and said, "You're strong too."

She said, "I have muscles."

Wayne hadn't been laid since high school and the last time had been in a field and he'd lost his hard-on. He hadn't been kissed since last June when he went to wing night at the Shantytown Firehall. Some local chick, there to play Bingo, probably forty years old, followed him outside to drink one of his beers and before he could hand her a can, she flicked her cigarette to the pavement and attacked him with her lips. He kissed but without a lot of sincerity.

Megan reached down and lifted the lid on the top pizza box. She reached inside and tugged out a slice and lifted it with both hands to her mouth and bit.

She said, "I'm sorry. I haven't eaten all day." She

took another bite and said, "Why didn't you go to college? I thought you were really smart. I was always sort of jealous of you."

"Really?" he said. "I'm smart but stupid too. I'm one of those dudes."

She said, "You were smart-smart, like Ivy League."

"I go to Allegheny East."

"You didn't want to go to main campus?"

He said, "No." He said, "Yeah." He said, "I don't know."

He wanted to say, "I'm broke."

He wanted to say, "My family is fucked up."

He wanted to say, "It's a hundred bucks to apply to an Ivy League school."

And, "The pizza shop is cool."

And, "They should let me do cocaine."

He wanted to say, "Do you do cocaine?" and, "Do you get stoned?" and, "I wish I still got stoned," and, "Am I ugly?" and, "I feel ugly," and, "You're so fucking hot," and, "Let me suck your toes," and, "I love you," and, "I love you."

She said, "AE is cool. I know some girls who party there on weekends."

Wayne said, "Yeah, it's fun," but he'd never partied there.

Megan said, "Branch campus," as if that explained everything.

He said, "Stress is weird for me," which was true but not something he wanted to say. "I'm probably transferring next semester," he said, which was a lie.

She said, "You live in Circleville, right? Any chance you could give me a ride?"

"Yeah, absolutely. Where is everyone?"

"They're downstairs. I guess Sherrie's parents still have their old house or they're not ready to move in here yet. They're probably waiting to meet with an interior designer or something. Look at this place. It's like Hollywood."

Wayne said, "What's her dad do?"

Megan said, "Rich people are gross."

She opened the pizza box and dropped the crust back in. She stared at the pie for a minute, moved the box, and checked the next pizza for toppings.

Wayne said, "So when do you need that ride?"

"Now, I guess. Are you going that way?"

He tried to think of how he could do this without involving his boss. If Mark spotted Megan, he'd ask a bunch of questions and ruin it.

Megan said, "I'll just yell downstairs and we can bail."

Wayne said, "I have deliveries still, like for hours."

She said, "That's cool."

He said, "I could swing back for you," but he didn't know when. The next order could be west towards North Versailles or north to Plum or Churchill.

The downstairs door opened and a girl who had huge boobs, presumably Sherrie, emerged from the basement. She was fat but possessed the confidence that rich fat people possessed. She strutted, doing a weird baby step. She lifted both tits like she was stretching her back then jiggled them like balls.

She said, "I'm so stoned, I could die." She said, "Look at my boobies bounce," and bounced her boobies. She said, "There you are, my little pizzas," and picked up the boxes like they were a small poodle and walked back downstairs.

Wayne said, "What the fuck was that?"

Megan said, "Huge boobs are a curse."

Wayne and Megan sat down on the carpet in the living room.

Wayne worried about deliveries.

He pretended not to.

He was willing to *not to* a lot to be closer to Megan.

Megan, amazing.

Megan, with the big brain.

Megan talked.

She kept talking.

Her mom worked as a waitress and wouldn't be home until at least three or four in the morning or not at all if she slept at her boyfriend's house.

Wayne said, "Your mom has a boyfriend?"

Megan said, "My mom is a whore."

She said, "No offense to whores."

Wayne considered all that.

He figured he didn't have to be home either, not for a while, not as long as he had pizzas to deliver. He would call home from Luigi's on his next pick up and leave a message with some lame excuse about why he was going to be later than usual.

Megan said, "Pizza delivery?" but like it was an insult to Wayne, like she knew Wayne was something more than pizza and the branch campus.

He said, "Yeah, I guess."

Megan worked part-time at an ice cream place. Even when it was busy, it was boring and you were stuck behind the counter. No travel. No knocking on doors. No weird people in their underwear, drinking cheap beer. She thought this would be fun.

She was thankful for the ride.

So they delivered, together.

Megan ducked down in the backseat when Wayne picked up pizzas from Luigi's. Inside, Mark had moved into a full-on cocaine explosion, tossing pizzas, dropping pizzas, inventing pizzas with bizarre combinations of toppings.

Wayne said, "You okay?"

Mark said, "Anchovy pickle."

Cara sat in the back, on a stack of sauce cans, eating pepperoni slices like potato chips, chugging Mt. Dew from a one-liter bottle.

She said, "There's the pussyboy."

Wayne smiled and said, "I am the pussy."

She said, "The pussy returns."

"It does."

"Okay, twat, be funny. Absorb the abuse. It won't work."

"I am a twat."

"You are *the* twat, not a twat, *the* twat, the memorial twat."

"The twat to end all twats."

Cara said, "You don't get to call yourself a twat. I call you a twat."

Wayne said, "I am the pussy to end all pussies. I just am."

"Bullshit," she said. "Stop that."

"Zen pussy," he said and walked out.

* * *

Riding away from an apartment in North Irwin, Megan pulled out a joint.

Wayne said, "Nice," and acted like he still smoked.

When the THC hit his brain, he could barely contain his joy. He reached for Megan's hand and she leaned into him, over the stick shift, so her head rested against his chest even while he shifted. Wayne felt beautiful in all of it.

* * *

It was twelve, then one, then two.

* * *

Megan had been considering the Peace Corps or Teach America, one of those places that treated you like a slave but gave you tuition. It was all so expensive. Her dad was nowhere to be found and her mom barely made enough to pay the bills. Maybe Megan would waitress or deliver pizzas or bartend or just stay in bed.

She said, "College looks like a pyramid scheme."

Wayne said, "I guess," though he wanted to believe in college, all the loans he'd taken out and was still taking, that he'd get a better job.

She said, "I like delivering pizzas. This is the shit."

Wayne said, "It's usually not this much fun."

Megan said, "Is being poor different once you get out of high school?"

Wayne said, "I don't know," because he didn't know, because he didn't think of himself as poor, not poor-poor, because poor was not something you escaped from. He was middle class, lower middle class, lowest middle class if anyone checked.

Megan said, "I hate living in an apartment. When I was in elementary school, my mom would never let me have friends over because she was embarrassed."

Wayne never imagined Megan as broke. Then he thought, ranking their spaces: lowest middle class, same as him, but maybe lower, lower than lowest, but he didn't quite believe it.

He said, "My mom is crazy. I think she has OCD or something."

Megan said, "Everyone has OCD now. It's the body's way of adjusting to its environment without collapsing. You count stuff. You have to wipe it down."

That made less sense.

But sounded smart.

Wayne said, "We should get autism." He made his voice mechanical and said, "I am Wayne. You are someone else. I cannot read the expressions on your face."

He thought this would be hilarious.

Megan said, "I don't think autistic people speak like robots," but still laughed.

* * *

They dropped their last pizza at three in the morning then cashed out at the store. Mark counted the money in the backroom with the door locked, blowing his nose and snorting. Wayne separated his tips and left the rest in a plastic bag outside the office door.

He knocked and said, "You okay in there?"

"Never better," Mark said.

Cara, sweeping up the kitchen, said, "Going home to suck your own dick?"

"Same as every night," Wayne said. "What about you?"

He wanted to grab a couple slices for Megan but he couldn't be near Cara, not even to step past her. The slices spun under a lamp. Cara stopped sweeping. She pulled the broom close to her chest and held it with both hands. She stood like she'd been punched by a fist bigger than her stomach.

Wayne started to turn.

Cara said, "Hey."

Wayne turned back.

He said, "What's up?"

Cara said, "I'm just joking when I call you names. I thought you knew that. I'm not just being a dickhead. You know that, right?"

"I do," he said, but he didn't.

"Being mean is just the way I flirt."

Cara looked at the oven, the heat still coming out so it bent the air. Wayne looked inside her body and where her heart was supposed to be, stood a small witch with a broom, sweeping blood into her veins. Her brain was bat wings, flapping.

Wayne said, "I left the car running."

Cara said, "Mark always tries to fuck me, not like aggressive, but like with the way he looks at me and stuff."

"I really did leave the car running," Wayne said, and moved but only slightly.

Cara said, "It's not a big deal."

He said, "We'll talk."

He said, "I have to go."

He said, "Soon."

He said, "You want a ride home?" and regretted it.

Cara dropped the broom so it landed with a thwack.

She said, "I don't know, maybe."

He said, "Shit, I can't. I completely forgot."

He said, "The car's running."

He said, "I have to go," and motioned with his thumb, there, away from Cara.

* * *

Megan wanted to go to Twin Lakes, even though it was cold, to watch the moon, to smoke more pot. They drove there, Megan holding Wayne's hands as he shifted.

At the lake they passed the pavilion and found the boardwalk and walked along the planks and threw rocks in the water. They sat and talked. Then they walked back and stood at the edge of the lake. Fish dove and splashed. Dry leaves moved with the wind. Wayne thought he heard deer. It was very dark. Small waves splashed against the rocks.

Wayne said, "Should we be here?"

A sign said the park closed at dusk.

Wayne said, "Cops."

Megan said, "Oh come on."

Megan was seventeen, still under-aged. Wayne always circled back to his failures. He put his hand on the railing and she took it. Pennsylvania had weird laws. There were curfews. Wayne couldn't explain any of this to anyone who would want answers.

Megan said, "You could kiss me."

Wayne said, "I could," and closed his eyes and waited to be kissed.

They kissed for a long time.

Wayne's body felt less like his body and more like the body he'd always wanted.

Then the sun was coming up.

The clouds were gray and mirrored on the surface of the lake.

* * *

They went back to Megan's empty apartment. Her mom slept at the boyfriend's house. How cool, Wayne thought. He tried to imagine his mom divorced, staying somewhere, having fun.

Megan said, "Sorry I live in a shithole."

Wayne said, "I like it."

The apartment was tiny and littered with take-out boxes and magazines. No one read magazines anymore. Wayne picked up an AARP magazine, wondered how old Megan's mom was, then set it back down. The living room had a couch but no chair or loveseat. A few paintings from Target hung on the walls but no Jesus stuff, no photos of Bible verses in cursive writing. It was more like a dumpy motel room than a house. They stepped over a hand-held vacuum cleaner the size of a small dog then walked to Megan's bedroom.

Megan yawned and said, "I'm exhausted."

Wayne said, "That was fun."

"It's still fun," Megan said.

They started to kiss, slowly, Wayne's eyes pulled as tight as he could get them. Then, slower than the kisses, they took off each other's shirts. Megan's bed stretched out on the floor, no frame, no headboard, the mattress covered in blankets but missing a sheet. They moved past the dresser and chest that didn't match and kissed more and stood on the bed and kissed and knelt and finally lay down and kept kissing until the kisses were pecks between drifts of sleep before they both passed out.

* * *

A little vaporizer sat on an old crate near the window and all night it hummed and floated tiny clouds. Wayne woke up and extended his arm across Megan's stomach. He felt like he should try something, that he should unzip Megan's jeans, that she expected him to make moves. She turned and, barely awake, trapped his hand under her thigh. He closed his eyes. A little skin can mean more than a lot of skin with the right person.

He hoped this was true.

* * *

He woke up on his back, Megan's leg across his stomach. He stayed still even though it was almost eleven o'clock and he'd never called home. The vaporizer gurgled like it was choking. Wayne slid from under Megan's leg and stood and put on his shirt.

Megan, barely opening her eyes, said, "Don't leave."

He said, "I have to. My folks are crazy."

She pulled the blanket from the floor and covered her tits but not completely. It was like a painting. She was like a painting, like a woman some guy in Italy about two hundred years ago would have made famous with his brush and oils. Maybe five hundred years ago. Maybe things never changed, that there was always someone naked and someone else admiring.

Wayne said, "You are really beautiful, like over-the-top beautiful," and he meant it and was embarrassed to say it because it'd come out as fast as a thought.

Megan said, "I'll kick the crazy right out of your parents."

"My dad's a lot bigger than you."

"But I'm tough," she said, her eyes still closed.

He dropped to his knees on the mattress and bounced and kissed her on the lips, on the cheek, in her hair.

She said, "Take my number," and gave him the digits, slowly, while he dug out his phone and touched the screen.

His phone had almost no numbers in it.

It was a shit phone.

Wayne stood again and his stomach growled, loud and long.

Megan sat up and said, "Did you hear that? Your stomach sounds like a garbage truck. Let's get breakfast," and stretched and lazily opened her eyes.

Wayne wanted breakfast.

She said, "I can pay. I have money."

Wayne, embarrassed, said, "No, I have money."

"Let's do it then. We'll eat eggs and all the bacon."

"My parents," Wayne said. Then, "I have your phone in my phone."

He said, "Your number."

He said, "I have it."

Megan said, "I'm okay with all this." She said, "You need to remember to look around. I think you forget you're always the smartest guy in the room."

Wayne said, "That's good?"

* * *

If his parents stayed for coffee and fellowship, they wouldn't be home until one, maybe two. Traffic was nothing. At the McDonalds drive-thru Wayne ordered the fish sandwich combo meal with a large fries and Coke.

The girl with the headphones said, "Would you like ketchup or any condiments?"

Wayne said, "Just salt."

But his parents had not stayed for coffee and fellowship. When Wayne opened the front door, his dad sat up from the couch he'd been sprawled out on, probably dozing. He rubbed his eye with his thumb, his oversized thumb.

Wayne regretted not calling with some made-up excuse. Even a lie that was obviously a lie would have helped.

His father said, "McDonalds? You're kidding me, right?"

He wore a Pirates baseball cap, an old one, flat on top and roped with yellow stripes. His hair, which was shaved on the sides and not much longer on top, the same cut he'd been wearing since his time in the Navy, peeked out from the cap. It was man hair, hair not to be noticed. He stretched then smoothed the front pockets of his jeans and pointed at the McDonalds bag.

Wayne said, "I was hungry. I worked late."

His dad said, "You worked late, bullshit."

Wayne's mother appeared from the hall.

She said, "I haven't slept."

Wayne said, "I'm sorry."

His father said, "I bet there's enough food in that McDonalds bag for exactly one person and I bet that person's name is Wayne."

Wayne said, "I thought you hated fast food."

Wayne's mom said, "No one hates fast food."

Wayne said, "You both hate fast food."

His father said, "Don't tell us what we hate."

His mother said, "I'm squeezing quarters, I'm so worried."

She wore church clothes, a white oxford shirt underneath a black dress with a white cardigan over the top. She bent to take off her shoes then set them on the dining room table. It was obvious she couldn't attend church without Wayne, that his father wouldn't allow it, but she looked pretty somehow, despite her puffy face, despite the make-up stain on her collar. She opened her hands and looked for the quarters, like they'd almost escaped, like they'd been out all night with Wayne.

Speaking to her husband she said, "Let him talk first." Then she said, "Wayne, do you know I almost called the cops? Do you understand I thought you were in jail?"

Wayne said, "Why would I be in jail?"

She said, "Where else would you be?"

Wayne's father sighed and walked across the room.

Wayne braced himself. He'd been slapped before, many times. He'd been choked. If he went back far enough in his memories, years, to elementary school, he'd been kicked in the ass so hard it bruised. He'd been beaten with a belt.

Wayne put both hands on the McDonald's bag. He held it there, below his waist, like it would block something, like he could use it as a club.

He said, "I didn't do anything."

His father leaned slowly into him like he was going to kiss Wayne on the neck. He came in like Megan had done so many times the night before but he stopped without making contact, without touch, his cheek past Wayne's cheek, almost past Wayne's ear.

Wayne did not breathe.

Then his father sniffed at Wayne like Wayne was a bad allergy, like he was shit, the opposite of how Megan breathed, the opposite of staying out all night. His dad sniffed again, twice, the second more obnoxiously loud than the first, then he stepped back and walked towards the kitchen, shaking his head.

"It's weed again," his father said.

Wayne said, "What?" trying to sound shocked.

In the kitchen Wayne's father opened a drawer then a cabinet.

Wayne looked at his mom.

To stand up to her husband would have been impossible, Wayne understood that, but she could have stopped walking and clutching coins and sighing like Wayne made her despise air, like she wanted to push it all from her mouth. Instead, she pulled a tissue from her dress and blew her nose, loudly. She stopped blowing her nose and folded the tissue and blew again.

"I hope it was worth it," she said, tissue still at her face.

Wayne's father stepped from the kitchen with a coffee mug the size of a soup bowl. He walked out of his way to come close to Wayne before sitting on the couch. He flicked on the TV. It was preachers.

He turned to Wayne and said, "You're dismissed."

Wayne didn't know if he was free to eat his fish sandwich or if he'd been kicked out of the house or if there was a beating still to be administered once everyone settled in and got fortified with coffee and ritual. The door to his bedroom stood open but his legs refused to move.

His father said, "Are you a moron now too?"

Wayne remembered to remember that he was the smartest person in the room.

His father sipped his coffee and said, "Will you please go somewhere?"

Wayne walked to his room slowly, holding the McDonalds bag in front of him, out of his parents' view. He sat down on his bed, his bed with a frame and a headboard and covered with a sheet, and he started to eat the French fries which were not hot but covered with salt. He stood up and pulled his phone from his pocket and found Megan's number.

Next time they'd do more.

They would talk and be without shirts and they would do other things too, kiss and touch and maybe fuck but maybe wait. He pushed his thumb to Megan's contact but hung up before it rang. He did it again then finished the French fries and held up the container and tipped it to his mouth to get the extra salt. In the other room Wayne's father said something to his mother but Wayne couldn't hear what.

SHE THROWS HERSELF FORWARD
TO STOP THE FALL

Judy down-shifts to second then up-shifts when the engine starts to rev. Her old Honda barely makes the speed limit and Pittsburgh is like a small misshapen mountain. One guy she works with said, "Pittsburgh is a city of tits," meaning the hills. Judy leans forward, motherfucking. At the top she pops the gearshift into neutral to save gas then coasts downhill, the road turning flat as she pulls away from Braddock, a mostly black neighborhood, and into Forest Hills, a white neighborhood where people live in fancy old brick houses.

Judy lives in Potowski, a tiny neighborhood filled with old people who sweep their front porches and pull weeds from the cracks in their driveways.

The light turns green and she accelerates onto the Parkway. The traffic is a disaster, always, no matter which way you head.

Judy has to be at work at nine. It's 8:56. Later, she has to be at school. She doesn't have any cigarettes. She loves cigarettes. It'll take a full ninety minutes to clean and get the fryers going before the lunch crowd trickles in. Her craving for nicotine is enormous.

Once, when she was fifteen and had been smoking

for three years but didn't have money for a pack of Camels, she chewed some of her brother's Skoal, long cut, the strands of tobacco wet as morning grass. She tapped the can like she'd seen older boys do. She took a pinch. "Suck it," her brother said. So she sucked it. The nicotine came and burned her mouth and calmed her nerves. She sucked some more. It was horrible but the buzz was immediate. Then the grains of snuff started to grow, to expand. She spit and made it worse. Her mouth filled with grime, like she'd licked a dirt road. She tried to get it out, using her tongue like a shovel. She spit again and choked. She dug with her finger but it was everywhere, gagging her, making it so she could barely breathe. She ran to the bathroom and locked the door. Her brother stood outside, laughing. The vomit raced up her throat like a fast car, something Judy still wants but can't afford. She spent the whole night in bed, spinning.

Judy does not talk to her brother anymore, technically her half-brother, but not for any particular reason. He lives in Montana or Wyoming, one of those states with mountains and people who want to overthrow the government.

Judy talks to her sister, technically her half-sister, who is nineteen. She works at the mall selling jewelry from a kiosk and lives with two roommates, a hippie chick who sells weed and her manager who is twenty-one. The manager sometimes climbs in bed with Judy's sister when he comes home stoned and hammered and lays there, breathing his manager breaths, not touching her. Then, when she doesn't respond, he stumbles to his own bed and pretends to forget he climbed under the covers fully-dressed with the co-worker who runs his business while he hangs at the food court and hits on the older Asian lady who runs Cashew Express.

Judy could not talk to her sister, like she does not talk to her brother, it would be fine, but she is happy when her sister stops at the restaurant with her ridiculous stories and man problems, looking for free fried food.

Judy downshifts again.

Someone could get rich by starting a company that delivers cigarettes, she thinks, Uberette or CigDash. She turns into the Crisp parking lot and rushes towards the store.

Her boss stands by the cash register with a bag of money. She nods at Judy and tosses the bag on the counter so it lands with a clang. Wanda is black but she calls everyone, even black people, whitey. She used to call everyone the n-word, unless she liked you then she swapped the er for a, but the district manager, also black, wrote her up. Wanda's gut hangs from her triple-XL work shirt which is wide but too short to cover the stretchmarks across her belly.

Wanda says, "Whitey, you late."

Judy says, "Come on."

Wanda says, "I know you know you late. Don't pretend."

The sounds of cars racing up and down Route 30, of people rushing to their jobs at the mall or at fast food places or chain hair salons, push through the windows of Crisp like white noise, something to sleep to.

Being awake makes Judy exhausted.

She said that once and Wanda said, "You retarded."

Now Wanda says, "I bet you about to apologize."

Judy says, "Do you see this?" and holds up the key to her 2002 Honda Civic. "This goes into the ignition of a car running on three cylinders that needs new tires. I poured a quart of oil into the engine to get here. I am without cigarettes." She pauses for effect and says, "Thank you for understanding."

Wanda says, "You still late."

Wanda gets to wear a brown shirt and a gold nametag. Judy wears a red shirt with her name stenciled in cursive on her left tit. The cursive writing makes her feel ridiculous, like a cowgirl, like someone who loves to line dance. She refuses to wear a hairnet unless the district manager is in the building. The boys on the afternoon shift wear baseball hats at sharp angles to look like sports stars.

Wanda says, "You always complain."

Judy says, "I don't have cigarettes. You can't imagine what that's like."

Wanda says, "You a drug addict. Take drugs, feel bad. Quit taking drugs, feel good. Sha-bam!" and she makes her fingers move like fireworks.

Judy says, "Cigarettes aren't drugs."

Wanda says, "I punched you in, not for you but for me. I'm tired of being the manager who has employees constantly punching in late."

"Fine."

"That shit shows up on reports."

Judy says, "Fine, I get it."

Wanda says, "Fine would be you coming in on time." Then, sweetly, "Your hair looks nice. Where you get that done?"

"Thanks," Judy says. "The barber school."

Wanda erupts with laughter and says, "You kidding?"

Judy says, "I'm not kidding."

Wanda says, "Oh my."

Judy rolls her eyes.

Nothing embarrasses her anymore.

Judy says, "I have to leave early to take my Art History final."

Wanda says, "The hell you do," and stops counting the money she unfolds into the registers in neat stacks.

Judy says, "I do."

"You go play *Animal House* on your own time."

Wanda assumes going to school is like a movie, four years of frat parties and hanging out in the dorms, weed smoking and cafeteria salad bars. It doesn't matter that Judy is older than Wanda, makes less money, and lives in an apartment that is basically a transient motel. Wanda treats Judy like a confused child, like a kid in high school, not someone taking out loans to make a better life. Wanda once asked, "They have hot tubs in college?" and Judy sighed and said, "No, Wanda, they do not have hot tubs in college," but they may have hot tubs at fancy colleges, Harvard or Penn State or wherever.

Now Judy says, "There's nothing I can do about it. It's a final."

Wanda says, "Bullshit."

"Please."

"Well, you don't."

Judy has an *A* in Art History. The class is not hard. She goes to Allegheny University but a branch campus in McKeesport. The professor cares less than Judy had imagined a professor could care. He never takes attendance. They never stay the whole period. He cancels random classes and seldom apologizes. Lots of students make good grades. Nobody studies. Judy studies a little. She just turned twenty-nine. Most of the students are teenagers. The older students transfer to main campus. By older, she means twenty. The boy who sits next to her, who is embarrassingly handsome, works as a plumber and talks about pipes and how much he hates wearing latex gloves.

Judy assumed being a plumber would have been a good job. One of her high school boyfriends is a welder and he owns a big house.

* * *

Judy looks at her watch. School is there. Work is here. She's bad at judging the distance between the two, not the miles but the realities, and her mistakes always piss someone off, someone like Wanda. It's ten o'clock. The fryers bubble. She needs the grade. If she keeps an *A* average, she receives a small scholarship that pays for her books.

She walks back to Wanda's office. The door is locked, like always. She imagines Wanda in there, checking out porn on her laptop. Everyone knows she loves skinny Asian chicks. Or maybe she's gambling. Wanda claims to make ten grand a year from playing cards online. Judy doesn't have a credit card to get online and the internet is awful. The women in porn are built so perfect they make her feel bad. She would like to kiss the twenty-year-old plumber from her Art class but it would make her feel foolish and she lacks time for whatever happens after kissing twenty-year-old boys which is probably porn or porn-like and humiliating.

"Open up," Judy says.

"Go away," Wanda says.

"I need the phone."

"Get a cell."

"My cell is dead."

Wanda opens the door. Her shirt is caught in the fold of her belly. Sweat lines her upper lip, like summer arrived but just under her nose.

Judy says, "Hot in there?"

Wanda says, "Phone calls on breaks. Not on my time."

Judy says, "Do you want me to stay or go to class?"

"Of course, you gonna stay, bitch," Wanda says. "You work here."

"Then I need to call my professor."

"Get a cell phone with a battery."

"Don't make me hate you."

Wanda says, "Please," then moves so Judy can use the phone.

Judy says, "Privacy?"

Wanda says, "Whatever."

The professor's name is Roberts. He is a fat man with a goatee who carries an old-timey metal lunch box and wears mismatched socks. He does not have tenure. Maybe he works part-time. He complains a lot about the administration, the pay rate, the hiring practices. Judy can't keep the titles straight—associate, adjunct, assistant. She thinks Roberts might be insane, like clinically, like committable. None of the other students seem to care. Judy dials the numbers and waits until he picks up.

She says, "Hi. This is Judy Powell. I'm in your 3:30 Art History class."

Professor Roberts says, "And you can't make the final today."

"Right."

"You know this is my cell? I don't have an office phone. I don't have an office."

Judy said, "I didn't know."

"Now you do."

"I apologize for not being able to make the final."

"Because your mom died," Professor Roberts says and snorts but not mean. "I understand. We'll work something out, grade-wise."

"My mom didn't die," Judy says. "I'm at work. I was

wondering if I could take the final with your night class. I'm sort of stuck here."

"Don't bother," he says.

"Don't bother what?" Judy says, trying to sound polite but worried.

"How are your grades?"

"All *A*'s," she says.

"You're fine. *A* for the final. *A* for the class."

"Really?"

"What's your name again?"

Judy repeats her name and adds a short physical description of herself and where she sits in the room and who she sits beside.

Professor Roberts says, "Sure. You're the older gal."

"I'm twenty-nine."

"Sure. You talk. You participate. You'll do fine."

"I don't know how to thank you."

Professor Roberts says, "Don't bother." Then, "Where do you work?"

"Crisp, the one on Route 30."

"Me too," he says and laughs.

"Me too what?"

"Me too, Crisp. I teach at the Crisp of universities. How much do they pay you? Are they hiring? I have skills."

Judy says, "Well—"

Professor Roberts coughs but away from the phone.

Judy forces an awkward laugh. She wonders if she should hang up, drive to campus, and take the test. Wanda would bitch but she would allow it. Judy is a good worker, despite her occasional lateness, despite her age.

"Maybe I should just come in," Judy says.

"I told you," he says. "You're fine." He says, "I love your macaroni and cheese bites. It's like there's real mac n' cheese inside the crispy taco thing. Your chicken is okay but it has to be the boneless. I'm too old for bones."

Judy says, "I'm glad you like our chicken."

"I like it all. You people don't pretend. You just fry the shit out of it. Everything. It's all fried," he says. "I've been teaching part-time at five colleges for almost thirty years."

"You're a great teacher," Judy lies.

"I used to be," he says. "I'm not anymore."

Judy says, "Thank you again," and the professor hangs up.

Wanda stands outside the door with a straw broom. She looks at Judy and shakes her head. The fryers rage and pop. It is, for the first half hour, a terrible smell, not like burnt feathers and gizzards exactly, but that's all that Judy ever thinks of, feathers and gizzards and chicken feet. Wanda extends the broom like a gift.

Judy says, "What?"

"Parking lot," Wanda says.

"With a kitchen broom?"

"Underneath the dumpster and around the curbs."

Judy says, "Christ," and takes the broom.

Wanda says, "Check my top desk drawer."

Judy says, "Why?" and thinks seedy thoughts about

gambling and porn.

Wanda says, "Fuck you then."

Neatly stacked piles of paper cover the desk. Wanda works like a machine, printing and filing. Judy bends and opens the drawer. Inside, between the neatly arranged paperclips and ink pens, an opened pack of Marlboro Reds lays flat on its back.

"For me?" Judy says, her eye practically twitching at the thought of smoke.

"I stole 'em off Keenan last night," Wanda says. "The boy's fucking fat. He don't need to smoke too. You be fat or you smoke, not both."

Judy says, "I could kiss you."

"How about you sweep instead?"

The hours go, despite the burning stink, despite the same stupid tasks. The old clock shaped like a red velvet cake says four o'clock, one hour until Judy can sign out. The customers, mostly drive-thru but some at the counter, keep coming. Judy rings and loads the meals onto trays and into bags. She sneak-ate three huge stuffed jalapeños earlier while Wanda took her break. She smoked all of Keenan's Marlboros. They were smooth and delicious, even though they were not her brand.

* * *

Later, at home, she calls her mother, Paula. Paula lives with a man who is not Judy's father, who bartends at a fancy hotel and disappears into his job every weekend. Judy thinks he is an alcoholic, functional but slurry at the end of the night.

Paula says, "Hey sweetheart."

Paula does not have a job. She's involved with a community center and sometimes teaches aerobics or pottery classes for older people. Once a week she drives the community van, taking disabled people to their appointments.

Judy says, "Everything okay?"

"Always busy, sweetie," Paula says, "you know me. I have no free time anymore. I wrote a letter to the *Post Gazette* about the shooting in Vegas. They won't publish it. They never publish my letters. They pretend to be a liberal paper but they're as conservative as the nutball *Trib*. What about you? Is the semester over?"

Judy speaks quietly because the walls in her apartment are thin and sometimes amplify the bottom end of people's voices.

Paula asks, "Why are you whispering?"

Judy says, "I was thinking of something, sorry."

"You should sleep more."

"I don't have time."

"You work too much," Paula says.

"I need money."

"Everyone needs money."

Paula and her boyfriend have both invited Judy to move in, "Rent free!" they say but Judy knows they would mooch her deeper into poverty. "Just bring us a little something," her mom says when Judy mentions stopping by and Paula means Chinese food with the extras, soup and dumplings, the wrinkly green beans. She means a pizza. She means cook for us and do the dishes. Her mom's boyfriend asks Judy to bring booze, his voice chiming in from the couch, "Tell her to get a quart of Jack Daniels." If he calls Judy himself, it gets worse, ice and mixers, chips and pretzels, and he never pays her back. One time Judy ended up driving the community van because her mom was hungover and an intellectually disabled woman needed to go to church. Paula said, "Aren't these people wonderful," meaning the woman but the woman criticized Judy's driving the whole way to Saint Michaels. Judy said, "Mom, I don't have time for this." Paula said, "No one has time, sweetie. Let's go to Designer Shoe Warehouse for their year-end sale."

Now Judy says, "I'll talk to you soon, Mom," regretting the call.

Nights are the worst when her bills are due and Judy is too tired to study for school and she remembers, again, how she doesn't have friends, not one, not a person her age who understands her and who she can understand.

She turns the clock on the crate by her bed so she can't see the numbers. The only thing to eat in the refrigerator is fat-free bologna.

To have friends requires money, money to do things, money to stop the worry of being invited to something and not being able to afford to go.

She dials her Aunt Lila.

Lila, who turned fifty-five last May, takes night classes at the community college and hopes to become an accountant. She used to drive a bus for the city but retired last year once she was fully vested in the pension plan. Now she wants to manage money, to not talk to people, to not drive anywhere. Some nights Judy quizzes her over the phone, checking the answers with a calculator.

Lila raised Judy for five years while Judy's mom went through a god phase and decided to become a missionary in New Guinea and give bibles to people who couldn't afford food, who couldn't grow food because of the drought. So much of this is embarrassing but Lila is the line Judy keeps from birth to present, never curving, always there. They say, "I love you," every time they hang up or walk away and every time they mean, "I love you." Judy knows she is okay, she is good, she can be better, all from Lila, not what Lila says but who she is. Judy knows she is not like her mom but like her dad, Lila's brother, who died the summer after high school in a car wreck after making Judy's mom pregnant. Judy does not ask a lot of questions about her father because, in her mind, she likes to make him who she needs him to be and he is forever eighteen and she is already twenty-nine. Soon she will be old enough to be her father's mother. Her favorite picture is the one from his graduation, cap and gown, smiling, valedictorian, smartest kid in his class, scholarship to Carnegie Mellon for engineering.

That's why she attends college now.

* * *

Maybe she should have gone to class and taken her final. She lights a Winston, her brand. The carpet in her apartment peels back from the walls. Little rubber pieces show through. She picks up her phone and dials the professor's number, remembering it's his cell, not his office. When his voicemail picks up, she gives her name and restates their earlier agreement: *A* for the final, *A* for the class.

Why the hell does she need art history?

Last semester she declared criminal justice as her major. The woman in advising said criminal justice would get Judy a job so Judy decided to be a cop, even if she isn't tough, because she is tough, not with muscles and punchers but she can push through anything and did and does.

* * *

The next day Wanda is in a mood.

"Not enough porn on the internet for that woman," one of the teenage boys jokes.

The lunch rush passes. The store empties. The tables need to be cleaned. The floors need to be mopped. Nobody wants to mop. Judy hates to mop and has no intention of mopping. She'd done the trash, the slimy bags, earlier, during a lull. The grease on the floor looks like wax, like polish. Wanda skates across the tiles in her brown tennis shoes to show what a mess the store is.

Judy holds two packs of cigarettes, one in her purse, one in her pocket.

She says, "I'll do the parking lot. I'm not mopping."

"You do the parking lot, you do the bathroom too," Keenan says. "Where's my cigarettes, you skinny old bitch?"

"Smoked 'em yesterday," Judy says.

"Real nice," Keenan says, but he smiles.

Wanda says, "I be in my office."

Keenan says, "You do that."

Keenan is seventeen. He attends high school half a day then comes here. Judy likes him. When he works the late shift, he closes the store in under fifteen minutes, twice as fast as anyone else. He places the big food order when Wanda is off. He knows how to read reports and he deals with the truck drivers when they show up early and block the parking lot. But he doesn't have any plans, except that he wants to buy Nike hightops with his name on the tongue. Judy wishes Keenan knew something, wishes he had a goal or a dream, so he would not have to go through what she's gone through, but he mostly smokes dope and eats macaroni and cheese. Weekend nights he drinks at his older brother's apartment or they go to clubs and Keenan uses his fake ID.

Wanda shuts her door.

Keenan fake-puffs at Judy, holding an imaginary joint with his fingers.

She says, "No, thank you."

Keenan says, "Old people can be fun. You should try."

Judy says, "Not this old person."

She never smokes dope and never did, not even in high school. She barely drinks now, just her birthday, with Aunt Lila, maybe a glass or two of wine.

If Judy makes it to the academy, when she graduates and gets her first cop job, she'll never use her gun and always let guys like Keenan, pot smokers and stumble drunks, walk away with a warning. The world needs fewer arrests and fewer people in jail. Not everyone needs to be put in a cage. Not everyone needs tasered and cuffed.

Wanda comes out and says, "I'm in a mood."

Judy says, "Everyone knows that."

Keenan waves Wanda off and says, "Go lose some money on the internet. Everything's taken care of out here."

Wanda turns towards her office.

Over her shoulder she says, "Clean this shit up, Whitey," and turns and slides a mop bucket toward the front of the store before closing the door and locking it.

Keenan says, "I hate when she calls me Whitey. It's not funny. She's getting so fucking fat, it's making her like a sped. The blubber goes right to her brain."

Judy says, "I'll be in the parking lot," and takes the push broom. "I'll do the bathroom when I get back, white boy."

Keenan says, "White this," and flips his long black middle finger. He says, "I mean, I love you old Judy, you're the best."

* * *

Wanda screams, "Judy!" from her office.

Judy screams back, "What?" and heads that way.

A small orange cone props open the office door. Judy kicks it aside. She leans in the doorway, careful not to see the screen of Wanda's laptop.

Wanda says, "You know why you're here?"

Judy says, "I do not."

Wanda shuffles papers into a perfect rectangle and makes a neat pile.

Judy never got her cigarette break. If she doesn't step outside and smoke one soon, she'll make a milkshake and hate herself.

Wanda swivels in her office chair and writes a number on the sales board. The number is worse than last year's sales and not even close to their goal. Wanda is shocked by this failing every day, ignoring the Quizno's and Popeye's and Subway which have opened within a mile in the last year and have taken Crisp's business.

Wanda caps the erasable marker and says, "Is Keenan stealing food?"

Judy says, "How would I know?"

Wanda half-spins her chair, serious.

Judy says, "Keenan is a good kid."

Wanda puts her hands behind her head so her shirt comes up.

She says, "You gonna bullshit me now?"

Then she leans back too far and the chair almost

tips. Her arms dart out to her sides like tiny wings on a baby bird just learning to fly.

Wanda says, "Whoo shit!" then throws herself forward to stop the fall.

Judy tries not to laugh because she's thrown herself forward many times to stop many falls, sometimes in Wanda's chair, one time behind the dumpster with a cigarette still dangling from her lips when a car raced around the bend.

Wanda rights herself. She fixes her shirt, covers her gut. She pretends to be comfortable. She folds her hands and places them on the desk like another stack of paper.

She says, "You almost made me fall."

Judy says, "I didn't."

"I ask you again: is Keenan stealing food?"

"I don't know."

"I'm watching you. I'm watching him. I'm watching his friends. I'm watching your friends. We got an inventory coming and I know we low."

"My friends don't come in here. I'm not in high school."

"Don't act like it then," Wanda says. "I know you give a biscuit to your sister before. I seen it from my office. She a skinny mall bitch."

"Whatever," Judy says, and takes her push broom and goes.

The parking lot is not getting swept, not again, not now.

Instead, Judy smokes three consecutive cigarettes

and flicks the butts at Wanda's Ford 500, a nice car, new, expensive looking with gold metallic paint that glitters. The restaurant blocks the afternoon sun so everywhere Judy stands is in the shade. She walks with the broom, not sweeping, and wonders what it would take to become a manager. Training? Paperwork? Blowing someone? Wanda grew up in a neighborhood where people murder each other over mistakes and she somehow made management but Judy is not Wanda, she is not focused like that, pushing ahead, stepping rough on anyone.

Judy earned her GED when she was sixteen and she enrolled in college nine years ago, always part-time. She guesses she'll graduate in two more years and maybe a summer. College is like buying a house one brick at a time.

She inhales deeply and considers becoming a manager, giving up her cop dreams. She has this thought sometimes and it scares her, how easy a car or a shirt or a pair of shoes makes her want to be someone she is not just to have things she does not need.

She will not fry food for the rest of her life.

She will not get pimples from the fryer like a 30-year-old teenager.

She will not steal biscuits.

She will not fry food for the rest of her life.

She will not.

Judy would like to smoke for the remainder of her shift but she hears Wanda inside, screaming. Keenan's voice comes over top, being defensive. Then it gets quiet. Then louder. Judy drops the broom to the cracked asphalt.

The Ford 500 looks even better up close, boxy and huge, like someone put an apartment on wheels. The interior is leather, pleather, something fancy, a beautiful brown, smooth and without the burn marks that dot the interior of Judy's dumpy ride, a wobbly bullet with the passenger door welded shut, permanently, and the mileage flipped twice. She presses harder against the window of Wanda's car, hoping to get a glimpse of the Ford's odometer but her breath clouds the glass and the odometer is probably digital, definitely digital, another thing Judy is twenty years behind on. She takes her shirt and starts to wipe away the fog. The air is cool enough to clean her lungs so she inhales from another Winston as she wipes the glass in a circle.

There is a cough, loud and deep, and it takes a second for Judy to realize the sound is not a customer but Wanda, Wanda who stands three feet away and holds her hands around the wooden handle of the broom like a neck she is about to wring.

Judy, without removing the cigarette from between her lips, stops cleaning the glass and says, "I'm sorry," so the cigarette bobs with each syllable.

Wanda extends the broom.

Judy steps away from the Ford 500.

She says, "I was just looking."

Wanda says, "You done?"

Clouds either move or stop, Judy can't tell. She releases the cigarette from between her teeth, from between her lips, and lets it fall from her mouth to the asphalt beneath her feet, the cherry ashes dusting her shoes.

"I'm done," Judy says, and sticks out her arm.

"Good," Wanda says.

Judy takes the broom.

IT'S NOT AS BAD AS IT WAS

Her boyfriend called from a crack house on the North Side and said, "Did you get my note about your grandfather dying?" He said, "I think I put it on the fridge. I don't know. Did we talk about this? I'm not as high as I sound."

Louise said, "Shane, slow down."

Shane said, "I can't."

"Did you say my grandfather died?"

"No. I don't know. You should call him."

Louise said, "Shane, you know I can't call my pap. He lives in a cabin without a phone. I have to drive out to Ligonier to see him."

"That's just fucking weird," Shane said. "That's some survivalist shit."

Louise said, "Shane, please," and stopped.

When Shane spoke, Louise couldn't think.

She needed to think.

Her pap's cabin was three hours away. It'd be dark and she wasn't sure she could recognize the turns. Her grandfather moved out of the city because he couldn't afford his apartment. Louise promised to visit every week and believed she would but she worked all weekend and three or four days during the week plus she took college classes. The drive was fifty miles up Route 30 and down the edge of the Laurel Mountains.

Louise paced the kitchen. She'd lived with Shane for two years, some of it good. They still had a phone with a cord. They hated TV. They hated the internet and music that sounded like robots. Louise still liked vinyl and her record player was German, a turntable in a wooden box her grandfather bought when he'd been stationed overseas and shipped home. She bought records for a dollar from Salvation Army. Shane bought paperback mystery novels for a quarter and read them in motels at night. He worked in computers and traveled to small towns he couldn't stand and collected salt and pepper shakers from the places he'd been stuck, like Athens, Illinois and Comstock, Virginia where he'd installed computer scorecards for a bowling alley that still had an original Pac Man in the lobby. Shane was a good worker when he worked. Together they were saving for a house. Louise desperately wanted one, a place to never leave. Louise calmed herself and said, "Shane, honey, did you just say my grandfather was dead? Think before you speak." She knew how to talk to him when he was like this even though she hated to talk to him when he was like this. She said, "I know you're not that high. Just talk to me. Listen to what I say and answer me. Think first. Did my grandfather die? Or is he dying? Is he sick?" She paused. She said, "I'm giving you too much information." She said, "First, is my pap dead? Just answer that."

Louise closed her eyes hard enough to hug her

grandfather, to wrap him up in darkness and keep him safe.

Shane said, "I think we talked about this. I didn't go to Ohio. I meant to write you a note before I left. I took some of the emergency money you keep in your underwear drawer but I'll put it back. Okay? Don't be mad."

Louise said, "I'm not mad."

"It's not stealing. I'm going to put it back."

"Okay, that's fine."

"I think I left my money card in a machine. I got some money and I think I forgot to grab the card and it got sucked back in. So I was just borrowing some money from your emergency pile. It was a loan. I meant to write you an IOU. Could you check the underwear drawer and see if I left the note?"

"It's not a problem."

"I'm in a crack house."

"I know."

She took the phone away from her ear and held it with both hands. She squatted down and leaned against the wall and stayed there. Louise imagined the inside of Shane's brain as smoke, as a glass bowl on fire. She knew the numbers of his bank account. All their savings were there, most of it his. He never bragged about money, how much more he made, or complained when she handed over twenty-nine dollars in tips after a Wednesday night when his quarterly bonus checks pushed two grand.

Louise had been napping, trying to rest between work and school, and now she felt what she always felt when she woke up: ashamed. Ashamed for resting. Ashamed for losing track of Shane. Ashamed for needing sleep, needing coffee, for standing up with the phone and walking to the cabinet and not asking Shane what needed to be asked because she couldn't focus without coffee because she never slept anymore.

Louise put the phone back up to her ear and mouth and said, "I'm here still. I'm just trying to think this through."

Shane said, "You're gonna be mad at me."

Louise said, "I'm not," and pulled down some old instant coffee, a single serving packet someone had given her as a sample.

Shane kept talking about Shane.

Louise microwaved some water in her favorite mug until it boiled. She mixed in the instant coffee and sugar and some milk to cool it down. She drank. Drinking coffee helped her stay calm.

Calm was essential.

If she panicked, it would overload Shane's circuits and he would react by getting higher or babbling more or becoming violent so she sipped the coffee and continued to believe her pap was alive, because he was alive, he had to be.

Shane said, "I get so stressed out. I do impulsive shit. I drink and I smoke crack. I fucking eat a whole bag of potato chips. I ate a cigarette once. I buy stupid stuff."

Louise said, "We'll work on all that."

"I know you're not going to love me anymore."

"That's not true."

Shane said, "I think I bought a new watch, like an old watch. I think I bought a stolen watch from this dude who was selling stolen watches."

Louise knew he was staring at his wrist, wondering if he could sell the hot watch he'd bought and make some money to buy more crack.

Shane said, "It looks like a Gucci."

Louise looked around the kitchen. The salt and pepper shakers were everywhere, on the counter, on the window ledge, on the toaster oven. One was shaped like a pineapple. Another one looked like a volcano. There were footballs. And Christmas trees. Shane wheezed into the phone. Louise picked up a shaker shaped like a baseball mitt from Toledo, Ohio, from their minor league ballpark. Louise loved baseball. Shane hated it, thought it was slow and boring. Two years she'd spent with a man who collected things from places he couldn't stand.

Shane said, "Do people still wear Gucci? I don't even know."

Louise closed her eyes and imagined her grandfather. He was old—gray and slightly stooped—but not sick. He ate bananas. He walked in the neighborhood. He walked in the woods. He drank one glass of red wine with the TV news at dinner. He took an aspirin at breakfast. "I'm moderate," her grandfather liked to say. "I'm in-between. Nobody's in-between anymore." Louise thought this was true. The middle had disappeared. Everybody was out there at the edges, pushing limits. Maybe that was all you needed to be important.

She opened her eyes and said, "Shane, tell me you're safe."

Shane said, "I get so lost. And I like it. I like being lost."

Louise said, "Tell me which house on the North Side. Is it behind the projects? Please tell me and I'll come and get you."

He said, "My lungs are burning. Other than that I think I'm okay. My lips are a little fried but that's to be expected."

The sound of his tongue wetting his lips traveled into Louise' ear.

He said, "Yeah, by the projects. It's the house by the houses that have been destroyed. It's not as bad as it was, though."

Louise tried to remember how long Shane had been gone. Today was Thursday. He usually left for a new job on Sunday night. If he didn't make Ohio, where he was supposed to get the registers online for a new pizza chain, he could have been in and out of their apartment fifty different times while Louise worked and schooled. He could have taken the call about her grandfather whenever.

She said, "Did you talk to my pap or did someone call about my pap? Was it a doctor?" Her pap didn't have a doctor. He hated hospitals. She paused to think who else would have called. No one else would have called but she pushed harder on her brain, palming her forehead. She said,

"Was it my sister? Did Helen try to get in touch?"

Louise wrapped the phone cord around her waist by slowly spinning across the kitchen. The tightness of the cord made her feel safe. Her grandfather made her feel safe. He was the only person she'd ever cared about who cared back. If her grandfather was dead, no one in the world would match her. She would forever be putting out to people who did not return in kind.

Shane said, "I should be scared but I'm not."

She said, "Don't be scared. Tell me where you are again."

"Crack makes you fearless."

"Where at on the North Side?"

"I'm worried about your grandfather."

"Me too."

"He's a good old dude."

"He is."

"Your family is all fucked up, you know that."

Louise said, "I don't know that," but she knew.

Her mom was somewhere, Portland maybe or Washington state. She took off with men. She'd done it for years. She told the men that her girls—Louise and her sister—were grown and fine on their own, even when Louise was still a teenager, even when she was twelve. Her mom sometimes raised these men's families until these men grew sick of her and realized she was not good at raising families, she was good at watching TV and drinking wine and buying stuff. Five years ago Louise had snooped around and found her mom and thought her mom had birthed another kid, a half-brother to Louise.

Then Louise quit looking because it was better to be searched for, to be found.

Her dad had never roamed, had never disappeared, but had never been much of a father either, and now and forever he stayed in the cemetery in Braddock under a puny stone. He'd worked for Volkswagen until they laid him off then he owned a van and some tools and drove around pretending to work. He'd fallen asleep in a trailer that he'd been heating with kerosene and suffocated during the fire.

Louise's mom skipped the funeral.

Louise attended.

No one knew how to contact Helen, Louise's sister.

Louise loved Helen but Helen was twelve years older and sane and driven. She'd moved away before Louise was in elementary school and, at nineteen, married a rich guy whose dad owned a trucking company. Helen worked as a dispatcher and her husband put her through college then she divorced him and moved to Ohio then Tennessee then Florida. She sometimes sent postcards before she took a job and moved farther away.

Twelve years was a lot between sisters, more than thousands of miles.

It was forty-five years between Louise and her pap but their distance pulled them closer, kept them coming back to each other. "We're pals," her pap liked to say and by pals he meant everything, the place for family when family failed.

Louise said, "Try to think, Shane, focus."

She heard Shane focus, his teeth clatter, a breath.

Louise said, "Was it my sister? Was it Helen? Did she leave a number?" She waited. She said, "Just take another breath and think."

She knew this sounded condescending.

She didn't mean it to.

She wanted to sound loving.

Loving was a strategy.

She said, "Big breath through your nose. Then out your mouth."

She did it herself, blowing into the phone for effect. Shane did it back.

She said, "Was it my sister? Was it Helen?"

Shane said, "I didn't know you had a sister."

She said, "You do know I have a sister. Please try."

"I'm not sure what I'm supposed to be trying at."

"Just try."

"At what?" he said. "What are you trying at?"

She walked to the refrigerator and looked for a note. Pictures and grocery lists and junk covered the yellow door. She moved magnets. She dropped things in the trash. Here she was with Shane on a picnic. Here they were at a bar, Shane smiling, Louise kissing him on the cheek. They looked normal. They looked happy. Louise remembered the outfit because she'd bought new panties to match her bra and Shane had taken them off with his teeth, being sexy, being funny. She couldn't find any note. She threw away a coupon. She'd made Dean's List last semester. The newspaper clipping listing the names was stuck to the freezer door. She added another magnet to the clipping so it would stay straight, so it would be permanent. She tossed out an old electric bill. She slid an old picture of her sister out from behind a coupon for Pep Boys.

Louise and Helen hadn't talked in years, maybe three, but there'd been missed phone calls and messages. She knew Helen was in Hawaii and that Helen had a good job managing a resort but she couldn't remember the resort's name and she didn't have Helen's address. Years ago Helen had said, "I'm running and I'm not coming back," and she'd invited Louise to come but Louise was not a runner. Louise was a stayer, an anchor. She would not leave her pap who had not left her and now she had, she'd lost him in his cabin.

Louise said, "Shane, tell me who called."

Shane said, "Let me find my lighter."

She said, "Was it my pap?"

Shane said, "Why the hell would I talk to your pap?" and coughed so hard he disconnected the call.

* * *

Louise was about to walk into a crack house on the North Side, behind the projects that always made the news for murder. Her pap's death moved underneath her feet and held up the crack house like bricks and wood. She knew this.

It was early evening. The sun was up but setting. Her car was parked, locked, and running. She'd hid her purse under a blanket in the trunk. The door remote was in her right front pocket. She was angry and sad and nervous but happy to be useful, even if it was only to be used by a user.

Was Shane a user?

He paid rent. He cooked Chinese on weekends. He fixed Louise's car and bought her new tires before her last inspection.

Louise paid her share of rent but she did not cook. She did not pay bills. She did not fix cars. She sometimes took Shane's dick in her mouth because she wanted to do something for him. When Shane did things to Louise, even things with his tongue, she thought of it as Shane doing something for himself or of Louise doing something for Shane.

Maybe Louise was the user.

Maybe it was everyone.

The porch awning had partially collapsed. The front bricks had been tagged then covered with white paint. It was a big house, probably three or four or five bedrooms, from when families stayed together. Some of the windows had been boarded. Other windows had been shattered, jagged edges and cardboard falling out. The house on the right had been bulldozed down to the foundation. On the other side: a burnt-out frame. The next house over lost its roof like a hat.

Louise knocked on the front door. Paint pieces fell from the wood. She started to knock again but she felt like an idiot and turned the knob. The door stuck. She tried her shoulder then her hip and the hinges moved and creaked. She stepped inside to the smell of burnt crack, mold, rotting lumber. Maybe piss. Definitely piss. The sunlight followed over her shoulder to make a shadow.

Shane sat in the corner on a tire somebody had tried to convert to a chair with old pillows and a Steelers throw. He was a twitchy mess. His left hand was buried down the front of his jeans, adjusting his nuts. This was his habit, especially when he was nervous or high. With his other hand he scratched his neck.

Another guy, a drunk or a doper, appeared to be passed out on a pile of laundry. Louise looked but didn't see anyone else. Forty-ounce bottles stuffed with unlit candles stood randomly around the room. Louise was scared but not really. She'd been here before. If you have to be in a crack house, be early.

When Shane, still seated, saw Louise, he opened his arms and said, "I'm so glad you came," but in a happy voice, a voice like this was a party and the drinks were free but no one else was any fun. She felt like Nick Carraway being welcomed by Gatsby. She hated that book. She hated classes that assigned novels from one hundred years ago. Who has time to read?

Shane put his hand back down his pants.

Louise stopped and said, "Please say something right for once."

He removed his hand from his nuts and popped

up. He walked across the room, still scratching his neck, still smiling. He was handsome with short brown hair and muscular arms from doing push-ups in motel rooms on nights when he promised himself he'd stay in and not drink. He was twenty-seven, eight years younger than Louise. He wore an earring and cologne when he was sober. It was late April. To her knowledge he hadn't been high since Christmas when he'd hammered thirty-five Budweiser cans in less than twenty-four hours and threw the TV remote at her head. Budweiser, she thought. Anyone who dated an addict knew: alcohol was the worst—the sloppy emotions, the promises slurred out between drinks. At least she could understand the words when he was on crack. The meaning was often lost but the words were sharp and enunciated.

He said, "God, I'm so sorry I had to call you like that."

He reached out and pulled her into his arms. He smelled like sweat and wet ashes, burnt flesh and something like toast. Without looking she knew his fingers were charred and his nails chewed off.

He said, "I knew you'd come," and wrapped her up.

She said, "Shane, you're hugging me in a crack house. Please let go."

He said, "I'm not going to not hug you because of a location."

She backed away but politely, like she needed space, like she'd come to him with a problem and now she needed to contemplate the advice he'd offered. He stepped with her like a dance. He was good at sensing distance and avoiding the respect it required.

He said, "I called work as soon as I knew I was going to get high. I'm not stupid. I said I had strep throat. I told them I'd make up the time this weekend. It's a pizza place in Ohio or Kentucky, I can't remember which. Did I tell you that? I'm doing something there with their registers, I think, I can't remember what."

She said, "I know," and waited for an in, her chance to talk.

Her grandfather had raised her. Her father had been a ghost, midnight shifts and daylight sleeping, until he moved into the trailer when she was eight. Then her mother started dating. Then her mother started marrying. Neither of which ever stopped.

Shane said, "I could get some more crack and we could go somewhere," and he made crack sound like an appetizer, like shrimp or cheese sticks. He said, "I don't have to be at work for thirty-six hours."

Louise said, "The first man my mom married after my dad was a pharmacist."

Shane said, "I thought she married a biker."

Louise said, "Sort of."

The pharmacist was a drug addict who sold pills to the Pagans, a local motorcycle gang. The Pagans broke the pharmacist's face. The pharmacist divorced Louise's mom for eating his supply. Then Louise's mom married a doctor. Or a male nurse. Or some medical professional. Then she dated another man while Louise stayed with her pap and ate the food he cooked in a frying pan and did the homework he thought was important and watched the movies he wanted to watch in black-and-white, mostly films starring Humphrey Bogart.

She put her palms to her eyes and pressed. The crack house—the smell or maybe the fear—kept her from crying. There was also anger, which she hated, how it always backed into her instead of out.

Shane said, "You look great, really."

Louise had thrown on a hoodie to wear because a hoodie felt like something she could wear to a crack house, like she was in a music video, like she was the star, only her hoodie was from the seconds rack at Gabriel Brothers and the zipper wouldn't zip.

Shane took her hands like he was about to propose.

He said, "I don't think you know how beautiful you are."

Louise looked down herself to see what Shane was seeing and the lines were not good. Her belly pressed against the elastic of her sweatpants. Her lungs hurt from cigarettes. She drank whole milk in her coffee and sometimes could feel it growing her chin until her whole face felt like it would explode with fatness. Her hair was in a ponytail. Her roots were pathetic. "To be loved one must love oneself," her mom used to say before hustling off to a champagne brunch with one of her drug-addicted men but Louise wanted to be loved without loving herself, to be loved for loving others.

Shane said, "I feel like you're mad at me. You feel completely distant."

Louise said, "Stop saying stupid shit, please."

"It's the crack. It's having a normalizing effect on me and it shouldn't."

"What does that even mean?"

"It means I love you. I'm fucked up."

Louise said, "I'm supposed to be at class."

Shane said, "I know and I'm sorry. You're a great student. You're the best student. I want to do better at work so I can pay your tuition, so you can finish. My parents paid for my school. I never studied when I was in college. I'm embarrassed by how much you study. You embarrass me with all the work you do. Honor Roll, babe. You made it. I never even came close."

She said, "Shut up, please."

He said, "I'm so proud of you."

* * *

Earlier that morning Louise had been offered a promotion from third assistant manager to second assistant manager at Bath and Body. It'd been a surprise, a pleasant one. She'd been pulled off the sales floor by another manager and led to the stock room by her elbow like she'd been busted for stealing but, instead of being fired, she was offered the promotion by her district manager, a woman who smelled like strawberry candles and could climb a ladder in high heels.

Louise, almost speechless, said, "Wow."

The district manager said, "Wow indeed."

They talked some details. Hours. New responsibilities. Louise waited to talk money. She already had a second job as a waitress. She had school. The district manager never mentioned money. Louise wondered if she was about to be promoted without being given a raise.

Louise, trying to mimic the district manager's language, probably sounding ridiculous, said, "And how will I be compensated?"

The district manager looked appalled, bolting back in her chair like Louise had tossed something at her, a bottle of off-brand lotion.

Louise, sensing her misstep, her professional bumble, tried to backtrack but she didn't know what to say and she knew she looked as appalled as the district manager or worse. How could you not discuss money when you talked about work? More hours and additional responsibilities for the same wage was a demotion.

The district manager leaned forward but did not speak, waiting.

Louise said, "I'm really flattered but I need to think about this."

The district manager said, "I guess we all should."

* * *

Shane said, "There are some things we need to work through,

obviously, but I'm not as bad as I seem." He said, "This may shock you but, sometimes, when I'm high, I get down and do push-ups, fifty at a time."

"I know," Louise said. Then, "I got offered a promotion today."

Shane, even more serious, said, "I don't want you to take it. Turn it down."

Louise said, "Why?"

"You're such a good student and when I finish this crack bender, I'm going to find a way to pay for your school. You think I'm joking but I'm serious as shit."

Right now Louise was missing her night class in psychology, an upper-level course. She forgot the title but it was something about education and the emotions behind how young students learn. She wanted to be a teacher. She loved kids. She wanted to be the kind of teacher she'd missed out on, the one who paid attention to the girls whose parents never showed up for conferences, who never brought in birthday treats.

Louise said, "I need that promotion," and she didn't mention that the district manager balked at a raise, that the promotion was a fake. She said, "Shane, you're not reliable," which was, somehow, not true.

Shane said, "You're right and I apologize for that. Do you know how much money I spent on crack on this bender?"

Louise didn't know.

Shane said, "I don't know either but I bet it was

enough to cover at least one of your classes this semester. I can do better. We can pay for this."

Louise said, "We're not talking about that."

He said, "I know we're not, baby, but we should be. You've been in college for almost five years, six years, whatever, that's crazy."

Louise said, "Nine years."

Shane said, "That long?"

Louise nodded.

Shane said, "That's fucked up."

Louise drove out to McKeesport to attend a branch campus because she thought the classes would be easier and maybe they were. The professors canceled a lot. The tests were sometimes open-book. Louise made a 4.0, perfect. She had at least two more years plus student teaching. The campus was nestled in a wooded area where deer sometimes wandered across the parking lot, where everything changed colors with the seasons. A small creek rolled underneath a crossing bridge made of wood and rusted metal. Between classes students stood and smoked and flicked their butts in the water. Redneck boys revved their truck engines in the parking lot.

Away from the college rows of projects dotted McKeesport so it looked like something from the evening news, from a TV crime drama. Nothing was made there anymore so the factories looked bombed out and the few stores remaining sold sodas and chips and lunchmeat and diapers. The bars all opened early and allowed people to carry their drinks in the streets. Louise knew Shane scored drugs in McKeesport. He showed up once while she studied in the cafeteria and his eyes shined like glowing rocks.

Now Shane said, "I feel like we've lost track of the thread."

Louise said, "You tell me what the thread is."

"That I want to pay your tuition," Shane said.

"No," Louise said. "My grandpa, you fuck."

"That again?"

"Shane, what happened with my pap and how did you find out?"

Shane said, "You don't have to talk so slow. I'm not that high."

She could feel the switch in Shane, the meanness coming.

She said, "I know you're not that high. I'm just upset. Work with me, please. I'm talking slow because I'm exhausted."

He said, "I'm not fucking retarded. You don't have to speak to me like I'm a sped. I'm not one of those kids you're gonna teach someday."

He made a retard face with his tongue flopped out.

She said, "Shane, I don't want to work with special-needs children. I want to teach elementary school. First grade. Normal kids. Maybe in a poor school district."

He said, "I thought you wanted to teach the speds."

No, Louise thought, I do not want to teach speds, I date a sped.

Shane walked back to his chair made of tires and sat down.

He said, "This is so difficult," and sprawled out.

Louise said, "Get up."

Shane said, "No."

He laced his arms across his chest. He extended his legs. Then he shifted. He uncrossed his arms and folded his legs back into his body. He pulled out his crack pipe, a piece of black glass, and put it to his lips. He went in his other pocket for a lighter.

Louise said, "Don't."

Shane said, "I wasn't going to," and set the crack pipe and his lighter on the floor like it was a can of soda, like it was a bowl of popcorn he'd pick at later.

Louise said, "Or do. Smoke crack. I don't care."

Other addicts walked around all the time, not using and not being assholes. Her dad paced his trailer until it burned him to death. Even her mom stayed in motion.

Louise said, "No, I do care."

She said, "Smoke the crack."

She said, "Do it."

She wanted to ask Shane why he stayed this way, not dying and not leaving, only she didn't know how to speak it out loud in a way that would get an answer so she reached for Shane and found her hands clenched around his throat. He was skinny but his neck was thick. It was muscular and wiry, like an oversized arm growing up from his chest, but she was strong and he was surprised. She dug in with her thumbs.

Shane said, "Louise, what the hell," in a scratchy gasp and fell back but Louise held tight, she pressed her thumbs deeper in the hollow of his throat.

Her father had drank and lazed himself to death in a nine-thousand-dollar trailer and her mother had dumped Louise to be stoned with strange men who would buy her houses but her grandfather, her beautiful grandfather, her loving pap, mill-worker and Korean War veteran, a man with callused hands and a beer gut, with a bald head and an unkempt beard, not educated past the sixth grade but smart as hell, her grandfather had taken her in like she was his own and he had loved her and raised her when no one else would, when Louise was one social worker away from being shipped to a foster home in the boonies or to an orphanage or to the streets to takes busses and beg for her life.

And now her pap was gone, he had to be, that was the truth of this, Shane took the call days ago when he'd stumbled into their apartment for money to buy drugs and the importance of the message still rattled his crack brain, dying or dead or buried, one of those, her beautiful grandfather, and Louise was stuck here in a crack house.

She might have said some of this to Shane or shouted it with her lungs flexed. She might have put her mouth to his ear and demanded answers to the things that mattered.

Or not.

She might have screamed in her head like she'd been doing her whole life.

A few seconds later Shane gained traction and reversed everything. He stood and choked Louise and demanded she explain what the fuck she was doing.

"Let go," she tried to say but the words barely made it through her constricted throat and out her mouth.

"You let go!" Shane said. "Huh? How do you like it, you crazy bitch?"

She pushed at his arms and slapped and chopped then finally pulled and got free. He backed away and stepped on a tire. He fell to one knee and bounced back up. He stood, not moving. She bent over and massaged her throat. On her clothes she could smell lotion, strawberries, candles, her promotion back at work.

She coughed and said, "Just tell me when the funeral is, please."

He was out of breath, his lungs heaving for crack.

He said, "How the fuck would I know when the funeral is?"

She said, "You know."

He took a huge raspy breath and said, "Yesterday, I guess."

Then she was lightning, three steps of flash, and she was choking him again and he, even with his desperate breathing, immediately turned and had her and this time, she thought, she was sure, he would not let go.

Shane said, "You don't fucking hit me! You don't hit me!"

Louise closed her eyes.

She relaxed.

So she quit in a crack house.

So she died to a man she hated.

She could feel her grandpa.

She could see his face.

But Shane lessened the choke, still holding her by her throat but not as tight, not as deadly. He shook her but not hard. He stood over her, keeping her from falling. He loosened then tightened his fingers, making her work to breathe.

Louise wanted to speak but could not make the effort.

Shane said, "You don't hit me."

He said, "I never hit you."

He said, "Are you fucking crazy?"

He said, "You need to apologize."

He said something else in another voice, one from across the room, and Louise opened her eyes and somehow turned her head and saw the man who had been passed out from booze or heroin or something else rise up from a pile of laundry and start to shout and dance. Shane kept choking Louise but the choke was like a hug, like he was keeping her close to protect her. The man shouted again. His arms flew over his head and he was coming towards Louise and Shane and he was dirty, Louise could see the dirt even in the dark, and he had long filthy hair and he wore a beige overcoat covered with coffee stains or oil stains or shit stains. His voice was that of a preacher, of a Baptist, of someone

Southern and righteous. He kept on, marching, raising his legs. Clumps of his beard were missing and his teeth were crooked and brown. He was loud but not angry. His shouts were of love, of brothers and sisters, and Louise knew he was an angel making it okay for her to die.

Shane said, "What the fuck is going on?"

The man said, "You cannot choke a woman! You cannot choke a woman! You must love your woman! You must love your woman!" until Shane relaxed his grip so that Louise could breathe freely and not like she was swallowing air in gulps.

The man said, "Now remove your hands from her throat and everything will be alright. You can make this love work again if you remove your hands from her throat," and he put his hands on Shane's arms but gently.

Louise added her hands and everyone slowly separated like this had all been choreographed, like this was a routine, and slowly she settled on the ground, free.

The man in the dirty clothes stepped back and said, "I thought you were cops at first because you're white but you're not cops."

The man was white so that sounded weird to Louise.

"We're not cops," Shane said, "Her pap died and she's angry with me."

The man said, "I see that."

Shane said, "She hit me," like he was pleading his case.

The man in the dirty clothes said, "I see that."

From the dirty floor Louise looked at Shane and knew this all made sense in the world they lived in. You build your own places. Louise believed that. This was hers.

The man in the dirty clothes nodded at Louise and bowed a little and said, "I'm sorry about your grandfather." He said, "I'm going to leave now. I'm sorry about your grandfather. I wish I knew a place that had electricity."

He turned and backed away.

Louise imagined a house, what she'd been saving for.

The man said, "It's not safe here for white people," and walked through the open door and slowly took the steps with a limp.

Louise crawled on her ass with her elbows until she could stand. She touched her neck and knew there were marks she'd have to cover. The front of her hoodie was torn. Her head was a bass line, pounding.

Shane said, "That was fucked up," still watching the man leave.

Outside it was night.

Streetlights tried to make the neighborhood safe and Louise heard cars and distant sirens. Inside the crack house, across the room, a light she hadn't noticed, a small lamp running off a car battery, shined a circle around itself. It was such a simple thing, such a practical way to stay out of the dark. Louise cleared her throat with great effort and pain and spit on the floor.

She did it again.

She'd never been beat up in a crack house before and

now she had.

Shane lingered, not coming close.

Shane said, "I'm sorry, Louise. I'm so sorry," and he started to weep.

He finally stepped towards her, like usual, like always, but she backed away, not because he would hurt her but because she would hurt him.

He said, "Louise."

She said, "Don't say my name."

He said, "Oh Louise, I can't help it. I say your name. It's what I do. I wake up every morning and I see you in bed and I know I'm going to get high. I can't stop it." He said, "Even when I'm not high, I know I'm high. In my mind," and he pointed two fingers to his temple to show where he was smoking crack when he wasn't smoking crack.

When she backed away, he crumbled to the floor.

"Oh Louise," he said.

His voice was mournful and overrun with tears and anguish and desperation but, more than that, it was still his voice, the voice of Shane, Shane on the floor, Shane drooling. Right now, at the Alcoholics Anonymous meetings in the church on the South Side, grown men with thirty years sobriety stood over folding chairs and said, "Hi, I'm an alcoholic," and if Shane somehow kicked all of this and managed to survive then that would be his voice too. In one year or five years or thirty years he would be able to stand up and say, "Hi, I'm Shane and I'm an alcoholic," which is what he meant when he said, "Oh Louise," which is what he meant when he said, "I love you," but there were so many other voices in the world saying so many other things, women singing in churches because they liked to sing, because they loved song, pastors preaching funerals no matter whose body, men talking over shovels and heavy machinery because graves needed to be dug, and her dead pap, voiceless but still with her, always, her dead pap stretched out in a metal box six feet deep in a soldiers' cemetery, the funeral paid for by the US government and attended by no one he knew.

JULEEN

Juleen wants to punch Max in the face.

  Max is twenty-two years old, a mountain bike dude.

  Juleen is thirty-three, five-months out of rehab.

  This morning, on the coffee table in the living room, Max left a bag of weed, two rolled joints, and six empty beer cans. This evening the daughter Juleen desperately wants back in her life is supposed to arrive at 6:00, dropped off by her father.

  The father is straight and steady and holds a good job in accounting.

  He never asks for child support.

  He never mentions that Juleen lives in a college apartment with a roommate named Max who leaves drugs on the table and eats Powerbars, who drinks energy drinks and wears sporty clothes, who majors in film studies and carries his phone around like a third hand.

  Juleen wears the same four outfits, sometimes washing them in the bathtub. She drinks water. She eats whatever, whenever. She majors in psychology because she does not know what else to major in. She does not smoke weed. When she did drugs, she did drugs. She never left her drugs on the table like loose change.

Max wants to make a movie on his phone, a documentary about mountain bike dudes, and premiere it at a coffeehouse.

Juleen owns a welfare phone filled with pictures of her daughter.

It's 3:00.

Juleen cut class to come home and redd-up, to wipe the sticky spots, to vacuum. The bathtub needs scrubbed and Juleen bought cleanser. She bought bubble bath because kids need baths, kids like bubbles. She bought a little lizard thing at the dollar store because lizard things are probably fun to play with in the bathtub and moms want their daughters to look at them and smile and squeeze plastic lizards filled with sudsy water and laugh.

The last time Juleen saw her daughter, they played at a park and some hippie girl let them throw her dog a Frisbee and Juleen wept in bed that night because her daughter loves dogs and Frisbees, because Juleen could not buy her daughter a dog, because she could not have a dog in her apartment, because she could maybe afford a Frisbee but maybe not.

After all these months of being sober Juleen is still Juleen and, of course, she had done these things to herself and, of course, these things made and make her pathetic as a mom, obviously, even as she only cares about the opposite now, please.

* * *

It's 3:05.

Juleen stands on the coffee table, palms flat against the ceiling, against the apartment above her, stretching her muscles from neck to toes. She says a prayer to whomever, to the ceiling. She doesn't believe in god despite the god stuff in rehab but she hopes, always hopes, because hope is a god too, more generous than most.

She jumps down.

She walks the living room, searching for Max's bike helmet, his backpack, his water bottle, anything to stomp into plastic dust and fabric, but he's taken it all to wherever, class or his job at the sub shop or to some trail he's pedaling on, sweating his boy sweat and not worrying.

Max always says, "Race the world. Don't let the world race you."

Juleen does not know what that means except Max does not have a child and his brain is a cloud of weed smoke and quotes from shitty Eastern philosophy books he pretends to read.

She steps back on the coffee table and places her palms flat on the ceiling.

Breathe motherfucker, she says, her mantra.

People—counselors, friends, even Max—think she wants to drink, to drug. They see the veins in her forehead and her neck muscles flexed and they think she will dive into a bottle or pop dope and fall into a couch, drooling. But she wants focus, not loss. She wants time and money so she can get happy the way people with time and money get happy, by playing with their daughters and taking their daughters to places that cost money, bounce houses and pizza parlors, the store at the mall where girls make their own teddy bears and kiss the plastic heart and place it in the bear's furry chest before they fill the body with stuffing that smells like vanilla cake. Parenting makes being a drug addict look inexpensive.

Being here, present, is easy.

Getting there is the crush.

Yesterday, Juleen stood in a grocery store for ten minutes, trying to decide whether to buy Fruit Circles or Fruit Loops, whether to save two dollars and lose the vitamins they pump into the name brand or to spend the two dollars and not buy the lizard bath toy.

Juleen steps on the plastic bag of weed and wants to punch Max in the face.

She pushes the ceiling again.

Forgive Max, he's a fucking kid.

Only one other person responded when Juleen was apartment hunting because fucking kids do not want to live with old ladies who are recovering from drugs and have a daughter and sometimes can't make the rent. Or, worse, they want to live with old ex-junkies because they are young and male and horny and one said, "You into orgies?" when Juleen showed up with her checkbook and said she was just out of rehab, trying to be honest, trying to imagine a dude in a Cleveland Cavaliers basketball jersey as a young adult.

"No, I am not into orgies," Juleen said, "but thanks."

"Me neither," the boy said, "but I could be," and winked.

Forgive all of them because they are young and terrible and Juleen was worse than all of them and she still wonders if she is better than anyone now.

Sometimes Max buys groceries and cooks Juleen dinner. He brings home subs for her and leaves them in the refrigerator with friendly notes. He bought her an alarm clock because her crappy phone does not have an alarm, because she did not know phones had alarms until Max showed her his iPhone one morning.

Do not punch Max in the face.

Do not.

* * *

Juleen first banged her daughter's father at a party one night when he was still in college and she was bartending at an afterhours club and sleeping all day. It was a fun thing, banging her daughter's father, like getting drunk or eating breakfast at three in the morning or banging a cute guy who'd only slept with one other girl in his life. Her daughter's father styled his hair with gel and wore shirts with collars. He asked questions, the right ones, he was interested, he cared. He was a sweetie, still is a sweetie. He loves his parents and his parents love him and they paid for his college and he thanked them profusely.

Now they help with the daughter and everything else, all of it.

They are good people.

Juleen can recognize good people.

She understands that she can be good people but that she is not but that she will be.

On the night they banged but before the banging, her daughter's father said, "What about your parents?" in his inquisitive way and Juleen said, "You're kidding?" and kissed him and took him by the hand to the back bedroom where they fucked on a pile of coats and he shivered and came in two minutes and apologized and offered to run out and buy them snacks.

When Juleen found out she was pregnant, she tracked him down and stopped by his apartment, embarrassed yet broke, planning to ask for money to pay for the abortion, half the abortion if he got weird, if he asked questions.

She said, "Sorry to show up like this."

He said, "I'm glad you did," and invited her in.

She said, "I'm pregnant."

He thought about that, not angrily, and said, "You're sure it's mine?"

Juleen said, "You're my one and only."

He sat down on his crummy college couch, which was nicer than the couch Juleen owns now, then slid to the floor and took a knee and asked her to marry him.

Juleen said, "Oh sweetie, get up," and helped him to his feet.

Juleen couldn't have gotten married because she still wanted to get fucked up. Getting fucked up was a lot of fun and it kept her from thinking about things like money and jobs and futures and dead parents. Imagine a boxing match. Imagine two hands, one made of whiskey and one made of cocaine. That's how Juleen fought the world. She believed in fists.

And now someone was offering a third hand, another way to fight.

Why had she never considered a baby?

Juleen said, "You really want this kid?"

He said, "Why wouldn't I?"

Juleen was glad she hadn't mentioned the abortion.

She didn't think men understood pregnancy, how babies were built.

She said, "So you want to have this with me?"

He said, "I'd be honored."

It took time for her daughter's father to understand they weren't getting married.

It took a longer time for Juleen to quit getting fucked up, like most of her pregnancy, like her baby could have been born with three heads and two toes, something she never plans to admit to anyone, ever.

No, she sometimes hears herself in her head, speaking to a panel of judges and doctors, I did not while I was with child.

* * *

Her daughter likes to be called Edie, not Edith. She's nine now. Juleen named her after a grandmother she'd imagined for herself when she was a child, when she was lonely, when she'd eaten all the peanut butter and the only can in the cabinet was sauerkraut and they barely had spoons, let alone a can opener.

In rehab, where they talked all the time, where she listened to people she couldn't stand, where they asked her to create a metaphor for her childhood, she said, "It was a big tire, a truck tire, and it was rolling downhill. I was the kid inside the tire. I don't know where the truck was." It was stupid, metaphors are, but her childhood was like that, spiraling, from birth until fourteen or fifteen, fun and scary and endless, one parent there, the other gone, then vice versa, then whoever her parents slept with, then foster care, then her mom, finally sober, who was lovely underneath the drugs. She managed to work two jobs and get Juleen through high school before breast cancer and fighting that and losing, no insurance, no money, being asked to leave the hospital then coming back the next day through the emergency-room doors where they had to treat her for another night, for at least a couple hours.

Juleen misses her mother every day, even the cokehead mother in the bathroom who chugged Nyquil to come down, but especially the loving mother, practical, sane, the mother who stacked small piles of cash on top of bills and a white envelope for groceries until everything was paid and the rest was their money to use for fun. Juleen wants to be fun. She learned fun from her mother. She learned sacrifice. Her mother white-knuckled sobriety and worked odd hours at terrible jobs—housecleaning, office cleaning, babysitting other people's kids—and still took Juleen for pizza then didn't eat any pizza so Juleen could take slices to school for lunch, pepperoni and cheese when they couldn't afford pepperoni, when they couldn't afford air.

At 3:10 Juleen decides to stop thinking about her mom then immediately decides she will punch Max in the face if he shows up but she will regret it and apologize and pretend like she hadn't meant to do it. Oops, fist, mistake.

Juleen goes back to remembering her mom.

When Juleen was fifteen, her mother said, "I could apologize every day for what I missed, and I'd be happy to say I'm sorry from morning until night if that's what you want, but for now let's push on, okay?" They stood in the kitchen, the refrigerator almost empty, the room dim and gray because they couldn't afford lightbulbs for every socket. Her mother said, "Just me and you, pushing on? I see you're wonderful and I hope a little bit rubs off on me."

Her mom said things like this, greeting card stuff, but she meant it, desperately.

For weeks Juleen had spoken less or not at all while thinking deeply on hating her mom because hate might have felt good, might have been right, because this reunion had happened so fast, her new mom not drinking or drugging or banging strangers with tattoos. Hate might have reversed time or paid cash or erased memories. Her friends hated their parents and their parents had money and took their children to eat in restaurants and bought them nice clothes.

Juleen never cared about those things but maybe she should have started. Or not. Being fifteen was awful. The sun shining pissed Juleen off but so did the moon and so did the fluorescent lights at school and math homework. Living everywhere, down to the religious foster parents who wouldn't let her shave her legs and their teenage son who walked around with his dick out, lurked inside Juleen's head like creeps on the street and she couldn't stop listening, no matter how happy she felt now, no matter how much she loved her mom, her mom off drugs and yammering like a self-help book.

Maybe Juleen was always a puncher.

She remembers wanting to hit her mom, to knock her out like a fist might revise a family, but instead Juleen invited her mom to a high school basketball game and they sat together, the two of them and not Juleen's friends. They ate popcorn. They drank flat soda in waxy Pepsi cups. Juleen said, "I love you, Mom," over the thump of boys in high-top sneakers and her mom said, "You're prettier than all those cheerleaders," and started to cry.

How sad to think Juleen's daughter will never know her grandmother.

How sad Juleen's mother disappeared from Juleen's life for nine of her first fifteen years.

How sad to look at the moon and not believe in gravity, what some junky told Juleen one night before puking in her purse.

The way Juleen forgave and still loves her mother,

she hopes so much for that.

* * *

Juleen buries the beer cans in the kitchen trash basket under an empty cereal box. She stands over the toilet, ready to drop the bag of weed, but she can't let go out of respect for people who struggle with respect, out of respect for other people's things, their interests, respect for Max, respect for druggies, respect for the sober, respect for anyone, for everyone, for herself when she'd spent so many years disrespecting everything, on purpose too.

She stuffs the drugs in Max's room, inside a wooden box he claims to have bought from a Navajo on a trip out west.

It's 3:30.

Then, somehow, it's 4:00.

Juleen goes down for a nap. She's exhausted but too tired to sleep. She still wants to punch Max, which troubles her.

She closes her eyes, thinking of Max's face and her fist.

She sleeps anyway.

* * *

It's 5:55.

Max stands inside the Ye Olde Teddy Bear Shoppe

in Irwin, looking at a wall of teddy bears. He's late. They called him in to work this morning after he'd stayed up all night binge-watching the History Channel's series on ancient Rome and smoking dope and sipping brews.

He'd planned to spend the whole day cleaning, helping Juleen get ready for her kid because Juleen had classes but they'd asked him to stay late at work, to slice the meat, then to cut potatoes into fries, then to clean one of the fryers because the other guys at Tubby's stand around and smoke dope and get the giggles but Max smokes dope and moves, he cleans and works and rides his bike and he studies, he studies hard.

Without the weed he'd be a nervous wreck.

The beer he could have probably done without.

An older lady, in a blue silky dress covered in roses, says, "Can I help you?"

Max says, "Yes." He says, "I don't know what I'm doing," and touches a teddy bear.

The older lady smiles and says, "Tell me her age, that's a good place to start."

Max says, "One is like eight or nine, and the other one is her mom. She's like thirty-five or something but she's been a total mess, only now she's really cool."

"Let me show you the matching bears," the woman says, and takes Max gently by the elbow and turns him to another display, bears small and large, side-by-side, dressed in fancy gowns, dressed in suits with bowties.

* * *

Juleen's daughter's father shows up in his Ford that looks like the luxury cars Juleen remembers people driving years ago, Lincolns and Cadillacs and Town Cars and all those big honkers she'd never been inside. Edie sits in the front seat, a first. It makes Juleen anxious. Juleen's car is a Hyundai, tiny, almost a pretend car, destroyable.

Her daughter's father steps out, shirt and tie, slacks, but disheveled, tired.

He says, "All ready?" smiling his dumb boy smile even though he's thirty now, a man.

"All ready," Juleen says. "When did she start riding in the front seat?"

"Blame the grandparents. My dad let her up here and there's no going back."

"She's so big," Juleen says and tries not to cry.

Edie reaches from the front seat to the backseat, gathering stuff, electronics and toys, her long blonde hair flopping over her head.

Juleen covers her eyes with her thumbs and rubs up.

Her daughter's father says, "Bag," and hands over Edie's bag then takes Juleen's hands and pulls her into a hug and holds her, the bag between them. He says, "Hey."

"Why are you so kind?" Juleen says.

"Because you're great," he says. "Edie has been begging to sleep over here."

Edie says, "Mom!" and sprints at Juleen, all the toys

still in the car, Edie's arms wide open like she's measuring the apartment, her parents, the love.

Juleen drops the bag and catches her daughter and lifts her and spins her, even though Edie is too big to spin, too big to keep off the ground, to keep in motion.

Juleen grabs again, lower, harder, the small of Edie's back, squeezing.

She says, "We're going to have the best time."

Edie says, "Spin me again," and her mom does.

LIFE SCIENCE

Around three in the morning at Allegheny East in McKeesport, a branch campus of Allegheny University in Pittsburgh, Eric Poliski, who everyone called the goth kid, who thought of himself as the goth kid, who grew up in McKeesport with a crackhead father and a mother addicted to shopping, who swore he would move to New York someday after flipping off every person in Western Pennsylvania who said he was gay, which he was not, he just liked fashion, he came back to his dorm room and decided to kill himself.

It was February. The snow had melted then froze, making it hard to trudge across the parking lot in his leather Rick Barkum boots without slipping.

Back in his dorm Eric turned on his computer and moved the speakers to the floor. He put on *Graceland* because, despite being goth, he loved Paul Simon. He took off his boots then his socks. He clipped his toenails. People worried about dying in clean underwear but it was your nails and hair they judged you by. Photos. Socials. He sat on his bed. The mattress was basically mush. He reached for the stereo and skipped to "Diamonds on the Soles of Her Shoes," his favorite song. He loved the melody, the way Paul Simon sang. He loved the lyrics and the story. The poor boy gets the rich girl and they both end up rich with diamonds on their shoes, theirs, not just hers. He thought that was what the song meant but maybe not. There were some African words at the beginning, some chants or a prayer, that he didn't understand, so maybe the song was about something else.

Eric was flunking three of his five classes. He hated his professors. None of those fuckers were Paul Simon. His poetry teacher said he wasn't allowed to write rhyming poems, like she knew shit, like she made the poetry rules and not the people with guitars who could actually fucking sing. She said, "Maybe read the books I assign and this will make more sense." He said, "Maybe listen to Paul fucking Simon and my poems will make more sense," and she walked away. His poetry professor was a twat.

He stood up and walked to the mirror.

He'd cut himself last year, not on his leg or the inside of his arm where no one could see, but across his face. He fingered the scar, wishing the line was bigger and deeper and more real. He'd used a razor blade and pressed lightly when he should have used something dull, like a screwdriver, like a corkscrew, and really forced the tip into his skin. The line above his eyebrow slashed down his forehead, skipped his eye, then started again on his cheek, but time and the sun had made it barely visible, more of a wrinkle than a scar.

He screamed at his face and walked back across the room.

If he could take the anger he put on everyone else

and reflect it back on himself then he could end the anger forever. He knew this but not the means to make it so, except by killing himself, which seemed obvious yet necessary.

He tried to make a noose from his bed sheet but he couldn't get the knot to slide. He was stoned on malt liquor and oxycontin. He loved oxycontin at least as much as Paul Simon. The first swigs of malt liquor always gagged him but the later sips warmed his tongue. He gave up on the bed sheet and decided to use his belt, a black leather strap with silver spikes. He made a loop and nailed the tail to his bed at a good height. He dropped the hammer. He loved hammers and nails, all kinds of tools, but he'd never learned to build anything. The fuckers back in shop class always called him a fag. He put his head through the loop and felt dizzy instantly, dizzy with all his air stuck inside him, which was what he wanted. He knelt down. He pulled with his throat. It went tight and he started to count the seconds.

At a party earlier in the evening, one he hadn't been invited to, he said, "I'm miserable because I have to be around people like you," to no one in particular. He said some version of that five or six or ten times, as many as it took to rile up the pleebs. The kids, mostly girls from the basketball team and a couple geeks from the sci-fi club, shouted him down then kicked him out when he wouldn't leave. "We didn't know he'd kill himself," one girl said. "We just thought he was mean."

The students on the newspaper thought about calling Eric emo as an inside joke but the editor wouldn't allow it.

The kid lived goth and he deserved to be remembered as goth. They could have just called him a creep. That was the consensus. He was a fake and a poseur and he'd masturbated with a noose. They'd never had a story like this. The editor called the police, both campus and state, and talked to various people and managed to get a copy of the report. They lifted some stuff from the *Tribune Review* and changed the wording so it wouldn't be plagiarism. They kept interviewing students. A sophomore reporter who worked part-time in Admissions found the goth kid's father's name and number and the sports editor called but no one answered. Other people said his mom was in jail, busted for stealing ten grand in clothes from some designer store. They went online and found a woman in the Allegheny County Jail with the same last name. No one felt like calling the prison or knew if prisoners were allowed to get calls.

The goth kid would have been twenty in March. Twenty was too young to die but really, after twenty, life was seldom worth living. The goth kid's roommate found him the next morning, still hanging, his feet turned bluish-black. He told the newspaper, "It didn't surprise me. I mean, he didn't like anyone. All he did was drink forties and that was it. And complain. He basically drank forties and complained. But he was a good dude, pretty much."

The whole campus, when they weren't joking about the goth kid who had hanged himself to Paul Simon, was pretty fucking sad.

Jana knew the goth kid a little.

She'd seen him at the Union, playing pool by himself. He wore headphones and sang like he didn't know people could hear him singing to get attention. She thought he looked like a rapist. She thought he looked like a guy who'd punch you for not liking Kanye. She read the story in the newspaper and talked about it with a couple friends. She called it a tragedy to be polite and refused to make jokes or laugh at the jokes other people told, mostly to be nice but also because she was having a crisis of her own about money, about tuition, about the money she'd paid for tuition and how she couldn't get it back.

After high school she'd worked full-time for thirty months straight to pay for college then started taking classes but still worked part-time, which was almost full-time, and her parents helped as best they could and she'd taken out student loans which she'd have to pay back whether she passed her classes or not.

A dead goth kid barely made a mark on the report card of her life.

Then, when Jana finally decided to do the right thing, when she came up with a plan and acted on it, her advisor said, "Honey, you can withdraw—basically, with the right forms—anytime you want to, but you can't get your tuition back."

Jana said, "What?" She said, "You're kidding, right?"

She'd been meaning to drop her classes and now she'd missed the deadline. She was furious no one had told her about the deadline or that such a deadline existed. The people who ran the college were crazy. They lived on some planet where money didn't matter, where people already knew what they needed to know about paying bills and refunds and deadlines but still attended college to learn about this shit.

Her advisor said, "Check your campus calendar, it's there."

Jana said, "Oh."

The office was lime green, like the walls at Western Psych where Jana visited a friend who cut her wrists the wrong way to get attention back in high school. The desk here was metal with a fake wooden top. Plaques hung on the back wall saying this woman was qualified, that she held degrees, but Jana didn't think so. She thought her advisor was more like the trash basket, cold and empty and industrial gray. On the corner of her desk was a framed list of all the things she'd learned in kindergarten and how those things would get her through life.

The advisor said, "It's an honest mistake, honey."

Jana was awkward with adults and she hated to stand up for herself. Her shoulders drooped and she tried to right her posture. She coughed but fake. She bottled and swirled all the furiousness around her stomach and head until she thought she would throw up in the advisor's garbage can or across her desk.

Jana said, "I screwed up," pretending to accept the blame.

She made a sad face, which felt more comfortable

than an angry face, and she hoped the advisor might see her sad face and be moved to act on it.

The advisor, an older woman, maybe fifty, fat, big-haired, wearing a sweater covered in lint balls, sighed and made her own face, a happy face, or maybe a sympathetic sad face, or maybe she looked bored. The fatness made her features hard to read.

Jana said, "I didn't know what I was doing."

The advisor said, "It's a learning experience. That's what college is about. If we don't fall, we never learn to get back up."

Jana said, "But this costs money."

The advisor said, "Yup, it does."

Jana said, "Oh."

Jana said, "Yeah, but—"

Jana said, "That's a really expensive way to fall."

The advisor said, "It really is," and opened a drawer and dropped in a form.

Halfway across campus, without a cigarette, craving, approaching an anxiety attack like she hadn't had since high school, her tongue dry as cafeteria bread, starting to shake, her lower back soaked in sweat despite the cold and the wind, Jana remembered the goth kid and how he'd killed himself to Paul Simon.

She thought: what about that loser's tuition?

She stopped on the bridge, rusted metal and old wood but fancy like the university had paid money to make it look dilapidated. Forty years ago they'd plopped this campus onto some old farmland and had the sense not to bulldoze all the trees but this was still the McKeesport where Jana grew up. Off campus, poor people lived in projects and less-poor people lived in houses with bars on their windows and people like Jana and her family moved to the next town over, White Oak, and lived in a tiny two-bedroom house that was at least safe and close to a grocery store without metal detectors.

Jana focused on the creek, the ice patches over the water.

She breathed deep, despite the temperature and how her lungs wanted tiny puffs of air. The dead goth kid knew things, important things, things he'd never use now that he was dead. His life, the death part, was a plan, some semblance of it. Jana assumed the university refunded his tuition to his parents or his grandparents or whoever was around and alive enough to accept the money because if your school made their students feel awful enough to commit suicide, the decent thing to do, the only thing to do, would be to apologize and offer a full refund. Anything else would end up on TV or the internet and wreck the university's reputation. Universities cared about stuff like that, public relations stuff.

Death required payback and apology.

Jana took off her backpack and found her smokes. She calmed. Seeing cigarettes did that. The wind dried her sweaty back and legs until she felt cold enough to move.

Her Life Science class had started fifteen minutes

ago. Jana didn't know what that meant, Life Science, if it was biology or a class on how to live with science or if it was a science class about living, which is why she'd never attended it. It was probably a scam, like she had a scam, like she was going to fake her own death, like now, like equal, like refund.

* * *

Jana couldn't call the admissions department at AUE and ask, "Do you refund tuition for suicides?" so she called a couple nearby universities. Policies for stuff like this, suicides and death and tuition refunds, would be the same across the board. She called St. Michael, a local Catholic college, and said, "My daughter was recently diagnosed with cancer and she's not going to be able to finish the semester," then she called Ben Franklin University and said, "My son was in a car wreck and it looks like he's not going to be able to finish the semester," and the answers verified what she'd hoped.

People were not so awful.

They just needed to be prodded with illness and death.

* * *

Nikki stood in the driveway, yelling.

"I'm not yelling," she said. "I'm speaking with conviction."

Nikki was Jana's mom.

Jana said, "Mom, please."

Nikki said, "Don't you *mom-please* me."

Jana stopped and pretended to listen, hoping to avoid a fight. Days remaining in the semester kept disappearing and she needed to act or she wasn't going to get her money back. A fake suicide took more courage than Jana had planned. Everything took courage. That was a class for college, not Life Science, not College Algebra or Geology. Courage was something to be learned. Suicide would be perfect when no one died and people cared.

The sun tried to make it morning but the sky stayed dark with clouds. It was winter, despite the occasional warm day.

Nikki said, "You stop. You listen to me."

She picked up a handful of snow and threw it at Jana, at her car. The ball dissolved before it hit anything.

Nikki said, "Shit."

Jana adjusted her backpack and sighed.

Jana said, "Come on, Mom. You're being ridiculous."

Nikki said, "You make me ridiculous."

Jana said, "I do not make you anything."

Nikki said, "You dress like a boy."

Jana had long brown hair, straight and thin, that she pulled back in a ponytail. True, she dressed like a guy most of the time in jeans and flannel shirts she'd picked up at the Salvation Army but she liked it that way, simple, pure, fuck off. She wasn't trans or anything her mom saw on the news. Jana knew she was pretty so she didn't have to be pretty.

Nikki had turned sixty-one in January, old enough to be a grandmother. Her hair was black with gray roots she refused to dye because the beauty parlors were a rip-off and the chemicals they used caused cancer. Life exhausted her and she talked about it and felt guilty for being a complainer. She'd been tired since Jana was in high school but the last months had been relentless. It was eight in the morning now. Nikki wore a robe. She'd never been outside in her robe, not even to get the mail. Jana felt bad for her mom but she also wanted her to shut up.

Jana said, "Mom, please, go inside. I'm going to school."

Nikki said, "It's eight in the morning."

"I know. I'm going to be late for class."

"But Jana, you came in at five."

"Why do you care? Who cares when I come in or how I dress?"

"I care, that's who."

If anything, Nikki should have praised Jana for being so responsible, for getting up after only two hours of sleep. Jana had showered and conditioned her hair. She had on clean panties, not the boxer shorts she sometimes wore, and she'd eaten a banana for the potassium. She'd brushed her teeth and used mouthwash.

Nikki said, "You need to do better."

Jana said, "I am doing better."

Nikki said, "You made me wear my robe in the driveway," and she reached down and packed more snow and shot-putted it at Jana.

"You throw like a girl."

Nikki said, "I am a girl," and she pushed her gray hair back.

"I love you, Mom. I'm going to be late."

Jana hated to fight and she loved her mom but not today, not much, or more, a ton of love, she couldn't tell. When Jana'd applied to college, she hadn't considered her mom in a bathrobe and snowboots or the extra hours at her job to pay for textbooks or the furious pace of commuting, work and school and home followed by home and work and school, and other things, buying pot to make the commute manageable, buying blunts and rolling papers and sandwiches to deal with the pot. She'd thought college would be like high school, only nicer and not as early, with kids who didn't wear designer clothes.

Nikki said, "You can't come in at five in the morning."

"Mom, I'm twenty years old."

"Exactly!"

"Exactly what?"

"Twenty years old, that. You are a child."

Jana said, "I am not a child. Don't say that. It makes me want to act like a child."

"You are acting like a child. Adults don't come in at five in the morning. Adults need sleep. They sleep so they can wake up and be adults again. It's what the world is."

Nikki untied her robe and tied it again. She stomped her puffy plastic boots so the wet snow fell away in clumps.

A beige scarf Jana hadn't noticed before popped out from somewhere and hung around her mom's neck. Nikki pushed it back into her robe and Jana saw her mom's bra, a white-ish gray strip of padded fabric.

Jana lied and said, "Mom, I'm doing good, you'll see."

Nikki said, "This is college. It costs money."

Jana said, "I know," and she knew.

College was the salad bar of bills, endless and outdated and not nearly as good for you as it appeared. It ate up money like the people Jana served at Hoss's Steak House ate up soup and lettuce and fake bacon bits.

"Mom," Jana said. "Please, okay, just stop yelling."

"I'm not yelling."

"Stop being a nebshit," Jana said, losing it.

Nikki clutched the collar on her robe and whisper-yelled, "You cannot call me a nebshit outside the house. You're embarrassing the family."

"It's twenty degrees," Jana said and motioned to the sky with her chin and turned to show the neighborhood. "No one is out. It's just you. Go back inside. I love you."

"If you loved me, you'd go to class," her mom said. "You'd study hard and bring home good grades."

"I am. I do," Jana said, but those were, of course, lies.

"I wish your father were here. He would strangle you."

"He would not strangle me."

Nikki stepped and leaned forward to be closer to Jana and said, "I know he wouldn't strangle you. He never could. That's why I do the things I do. That's why I have to fight you. Your father babies you."

Jana knew her father was on his first coffee break. She knew, if he were here, he'd move Nikki inside by the shoulders, gently, lovingly, so Jana could drive to school.

Nikki said, "I'd cry but my tears would freeze."

Jana climbed into her car, an old Ford Windstar, a minivan she'd inherited from her uncle. Empty Dunkin Donuts coffee cups covered the front passenger seat. The ashtray overflowed with cigarette butts. Jana found her keys in the ignition. A snow-streaked version of her mom hugged her bath-robed shoulders through the windshield and pouted.

Nikki pointed and said, "Scrape your windshield."

Jana couldn't wait to die, to take a bunch of pills and nap and wake up and organize her life into something she could use.

Nikki said, "The windshield is all icy."

Jana turned the key in the Windstar then turned it again but nothing happened, not a chug. She stepped on the gas, pumping the pedal. She started to pray and felt stupid.

She said, "Please," and tried again.

She looked at the radio and pushed the dial then flicked her high beams then turned on the overhead light but nothing sang or lit.

Nikki walked around the car and tapped Jana's window.

Jana put her face on the steering wheel.

"I'll get the jumper cables," her mom said, through the glass.

* * *

On the way to campus Jana stopped at a beer distributor that served minors and bought a case of Coors Light in cans because she couldn't afford bottles. She made it to Linda's place and parked. She pulled the case from the passenger seat and hefted it to her shoulder, a brick of beer. Jana slammed the car door shut with her foot and Linda waved from the porch.

Linda was Jana's best friend.

Everyone called her Linda X because she'd made a porno with an old boyfriend and the boyfriend had passed it around, phone to phone, some creepy internet site, but Jana called her Linda, just Linda, because Linda said, "That's behind me," and Jana believed her. Linda could make a porno and get beyond it because she was fun but serious. Smart. Beyond smart. She attended classes, even the ones she hated, and played intramural volleyball to stay in shape and she only ate one meal a day, always with a salad, and when she snacked, even stoned, she munched on an apple or some carrot sticks.

Linda said, "You're late. I'm going to miss my 9:30."

Jana said, "You have forty-five minutes."

Linda said, "I like to be early," and smiled.

Linda was older, twenty-four. She'd enlisted in the

Navy for four years, earning tuition money while sailing around the Middle East. Jana couldn't have lived on a boat and she was scared of Arab people and their religion, even just floating around their countries, so she didn't know why she and Linda liked each other but they did. Jana admired that Linda refused to be wrecked. In a couple years she hoped to be like that.

Linda said, "Hustle it up, bitch."

Jana climbed the concrete slabs leading to the front porch. Her legs pinged, like when she used to exercise. She breathed deep, trying to calm her heart and lungs, and wished for a cigarette. She moved the case to her belly like she was cradling a toddler.

Linda reached for the case and Jana handed it over.

Linda said, "There's a fat man inside your little body."

"I know," Jana said, "and he doesn't dress well either."

Linda dressed in an outfit from the H.H.Large. Her sweater matched her knit hat which matched her socks. Her hair, the little bit that showed, ended in loose curls. She wore make-up, a fancy nighttime face for a club, and her nails were polished. How someone so girly could survive in the military Jana didn't understand, but Linda said lots of the women in the Navy were like that. One girl had managed to shave her legs during basics, hiding a razor in Freedom Hall where they met up and did calisthenics before morning runs.

Linda's apartment was tiny but neat, in a corner away from the larger places. She lived alone, almost unheard of, and kept food in her cabinets and the bathroom was always clean. Some pictures, mostly movie stars, mostly Johnny Depp, held onto the refrigerator with magnets. The military still paid Linda but Jana didn't know how much. Linda's coffee cups matched.

Linda said, "Are you sure you want to do this? It's a little extreme."

Jana said, "Tuition prices are extreme."

"I'm afraid something will go wrong."

"What could go wrong?"

"You could die."

Jana said, "Fuck that."

Linda picked up her purse. She was serious about being early for class.

Jana said, "How do you do it, going to class? You don't even have a major."

"How can I decide what to major in if I don't go to class?"

Jana said, "That's creepy logic, I think," as she tore open the cardboard on the case of Coors Light and reached inside for a beer, which she immediately chugged.

Linda said, "It's philosophy. I like it. It's Sartre. He was famous and got to bang a lot of women even though he looked like a troll. His wife-partner-person didn't even care. To be that ugly and to get laid all the time means something. I knew dudes like that in the Navy. Hot chicks would wave panties at their fat ugly faces."

"That's the whole class?"

"There are ideas too but they're harder to understand.

I like the biographies."

Jana said, "I think you banged a couple trolls when you were in the Navy and that class makes you feel better," and cracked open another beer.

"More than a couple," Linda said. "We all have our weaknesses. I liked gross dudes with big hearts. You're drinking warm beer for breakfast."

"It's only a little warm," Jana said. "What is philosophy anyway? I mean, what is the real subject of the class? Like, the philosophy of what?"

Linda said, "I don't know. I just like it. It's okay to like things. You should like things. I like massages. I like getting my nails done." She extended her fingers, the perfect pink tips, then tapped out a beat on the table. She said, "How much sleep did you get last night? I left at eleven and you were just getting started."

"Not much."

"Did you bang Trevor?"

"I didn't even talk to Trevor."

"I saw you making out with Trevor on the couch."

"That wasn't me."

"I wish it was me," Linda said. "He's cute for a little scuzbucket boy. That's the best thing about coming back to college late—you get to meet all these boys before they have guts and man-boobs. A guy hits twenty-five and he's done."

Linda lifted her tits, held them, then dropped them and followed with her head and shoulders so she was hunched over, gut extended, like gravity was age, like she'd deteriorated into a schlubbie male in seconds.

Jana said, "Twenty-five's not that old."

"You'll see. How old is Trevor, like nineteen?"

"I don't know, something like that."

Tattoos covered Trevor's arms. He cut his own hair with a razor blade. Weekends, he painted houses with his uncle and claimed to spend all his paychecks on weed and maybe he did. He was always stoned, always red-eyed and smirky.

Linda said, "Someone told me Trevor has a big dick."

Jana said, "That stuff doesn't matter."

"It most definitely does," Linda said, and looked appalled.

Big dick or not, Trevor was cute, mostly because of the house painting and the drugs, but Jana had morals and Trevor was aggressive like a high school boy, like the skinny drum major who tried to touch Jana's pussy on the band bus when they were sitting three in a seat. The little motherfucker had hands like racecars going up the back of Jana's shirt and every time she blocked him he took another lane, up the side of her shirt, down the back of her pants, straight for her crotch. Trevor was like that, like the Kung Fu version of that, hands everywhere, except he was a good kisser, except paint splatters covered his jeans and boots. Jana decided to take a nap while kissing Trevor, just rest her tongue in his mouth so she could regroup and energize, and when she woke up ten seconds later he was massaging her ass crack.

You didn't just go for someone's ass crack at a party.

Ass cracks were private.

Linda said, "You ever kiss a chick?"

Jana said, "What? No," and her neck lit up with red like she'd turned on a stoplight in her throat. She said, "Don't be perverted," the heat crumbling her words because she'd kissed a girl once, drunk, visiting Kent State with a friend whose sister went there.

"Liar."

"What?"

"You just turned ten shades of red," Linda said. "You lying carpet muncher."

"What?"

"You are a woman of leisure."

Jana said, "Is that like a dyke?"

She looked at the refrigerator and noticed three postcards of women, two in bikinis, all of them suddenly looking a little bi, and a glamour shot of Johnny Depp when he was young, looking like a woman.

Linda said, "I let a chick go down on me once in a three-way."

Jana said, "Eww gross," and felt like a sixth grader, like a prude.

In seventh grade she slept with a ninth grader and felt so bad about the pain and the nakedness and the blood on his mom's bed, she started to cry and he stopped and wouldn't start again even though she kept telling him she was fine, to keep going. She waited until ninth grade to kiss a boy again and that summer the same boy went down on her in a field and Jana felt so embarrassed she wanted to cry, like crying was her thing when it came to sex, it was a terrible feeling, like a black wave, then somehow she came and didn't cry and fell in love and spent the rest of that summer coming in cars parked on backroads and at a ballfield when no one was around and she learned to make the boy come and she loved that too but then he left her to have an affair with a middle-aged woman with two kids who managed a JoAnn Fabrics.

Not much good, sexually speaking, had happened since.

Linda said, "Look how fake you are, you box eater. It makes me love you even more, you fucking rug muncher. You're gonna marry a chick and be so happy one day."

"I just drink too much because I'm a social loser."

"You always look so worried. Be happy."

Jana said, "My mom worries. I inherited it from her."

Linda said, "Class calls."

Jana opened her third beer and said, "Where's the pills?"

"The pills are hidden away. I don't feel like digging them up."

"Skip class," Jana said.

"This is college, you go to class."

"Most college students would disagree."

"Not the smart ones."

Even if Linda couldn't tell what the Navy had

done to her brain, not fried it exactly but altered it in some subtle way, Jana knew. She saw it in Linda's posture, in the way she constantly checked her phone for the time. Linda could do anything—class, studying, singing in the school's embarrassing musical about Betsy Ross—without thinking. She simply did because you were supposed to do. The Navy taught her that, how to follow. This made Jana furious and confused and slightly jealous.

Linda said, "Why don't you just run screaming across campus? Act all fucking mental. Take a shit on the bridge. How can they prove you're not crazy?"

Jana said, "Pills, please," and burped as loud as she could and crushed the beer can like she was a steel worker or her dad.

"Come on," Linda said. "This isn't funny."

To pretend to die was a joke but as soon as Jana had said the word *pills*, the humor stopped and her stomach twisted and she could feel her insides, her lungs getting skinny, her heart beating double. It was so fierce, her tailbone hurt.

College did this, not Jana.

It killed that goth kid and now Jana had to pretend to follow while he rotted under a tiny tombstone in the cemetery in East Pittsburgh where underaged kids partied and dropped beer cans on his grave, where an alcoholic dude in a t-shirt making minimum wage would plant a flower next Spring before he went back to cutting grass.

Weeks ago, hoping for a miracle, hoping to avoid

this, Jana'd gone back to see another advisor and this advisor, a young man, a kid really, dressed in faded slacks and a bad tie, said, "Withdrawal was four weeks ago and that was for half tuition."

Jana, just off her shift, smelling like burnt meat, like bleach, wanting help, desperate, clumsy as usual, said, "But I work at a steak house."

The advisor said, "Yeah, cool."

* * *

Linda came back with the pills, a whole bottle of oxycontin. She'd had knee surgery a year ago but the pain wasn't as bad as the doctor had suspected and she'd saved most of the drugs, not for Jana to OD on, but still.

Jana said, "How many do I take? All of them?"

Linda said, "Give me those," and handed out four pills.

Jana said, "This is not going to kill me."

"It's not supposed to kill you."

"But we have to make it look good."

Linda said, "Fine, I have to go, take as many as you want." She picked up her purse and started to leave. Then she stopped. She looked at Jana and her face changed, like she might cry. She said, "I'm sorry. You shouldn't have to do this. The world is way more fucked up than it should be. It should be better."

Jana said, "You're my best friend."

Linda said, "I'll stay," and put her purse down but Jana couldn't have stood for that any more than she could have stood for losing her full tuition.

Jana said, "Go."

* * *

Jana dreamed with her eyes open and liked it, the way she could pick the people who passed through her subconscious or conscious or whatever, even though they seemed to do what they wanted in the dream she was creating. She'd chugged two more beers and taken five pills then five more. She didn't know if that was too much or too little. Ten pills seemed moderate, slightly more because Jana was small, which was what she wanted, slightly more, too much, realistic.

She flipped through TV channels. Linda didn't have cable so it was just news coming through the fuzz and women talking about the world in a way that was supposed to make sense. Sense had passed. Jana knew that.

She stood up.

The pills pushed her down.

She stood up again, ready for the sensation.

Her legs moved like they were filled with concrete, not all concrete but concrete and something else, maybe feathers. Her heart beat slowly and randomly like it was on break, like it was playing a heart for fun, at intramurals, pumping occasionally like a drunk girl hitting volleyballs.

Jana blinked. Her eyes wouldn't focus but in a good way, like she could only see the outline of death and not death itself.

She sat back down but not on purpose, a gentle falling.

She thought for a second she wasn't breathing.

The air had not disappeared but turned invisible.

She felt panicked, sure that she'd taken too many pills, but then the panic jolted her out of the sluggishness and she stood and walked across the room. Her heart beat fine. She turned off the TV. She listened to her breathing and it was there, slow and raspy but definitely present. She pulled a Coors Light from the box. She steadied herself and stepped thoughtfully to the kitchen and grabbed the cordless phone. She didn't plan on calling 911—that was Linda's job—but having the phone made her feel safe.

Time passed.

Time passed again.

Even though it was winter, the overhead fan did circles. Jana liked the sound, the gentle whir. When she opened her eyes, she realized she'd spilled beer in her lap. She didn't know where to move the can without standing and she didn't feel like standing, concrete legs, feathers, so she left it there, the beer in her lap, like she'd pissed herself.

And she'd specifically worn clean underwear and a nice bra.

More time.

And more time.

Jana closed her eyes to think about her father, to talk

to her father, directly.

He'd worked in a factory, a little one, not the big ones like in the movies and on the news. This was a shop, that's what he called it. Jana loved her dad. He wore grease like a uniform, like designer clothes, something cool and that you were proud of. Jana cut his fingernails sometimes, asked to cut his fingernails. They were so greasy and he was so tired. He stretched out on the bed. She stood above him. "Fingernails don't matter," he'd say and Jana would push the cuticles, gently, then she would take off his socks and cut his toenails, little slices of white wood and grease. She'd touch his forehead.

"Be gentle," her father said, when she cut flesh, but not mean.

She said, "I'm trying."

He said, "I know you are, sweetie," and tucked a pillow under his head.

* * *

Jana said, "Dad, I love you," like he was here, because he was, somehow, the drugs, the love, and she worked another pill from the orange container on the end table and swallowed it dry.

She didn't think she could stand again.

Her dad ate bologna and mustard on white beard.

He did something with sheet metal.

He did something with a press.

He stared at her and worried about the pills.

He worried about everything.

He loved his daughter so much.

Jana looked at the TV which was not on but maybe moving, just the screen.

Her dad prefaced everything he said with, "It's not like when I was young," and touched her shoulder and moved on without completing his thought, without delivering advice or criticism. Nervous, he cleaned his fingernails, the ones Jana had always cut, and said, "Forbes magazine says nursing is a growing field. Are you interested in nursing?" Sometimes, he ate salami without bread, rolled up, and he talked with his mouth full. Now, he said, "What about teaching? That's a noble profession."

Jana said, "We can talk," but her dad's mouth was stuffed.

He stood in the TV, like he was on a cop show, but a cop show with mill workers, shop guys, some other crumpled men eating bologna.

Jana knew the dream was a dream, as she chose it to be, a space to think where she could almost direct, but she still felt embarrassed by the other men on the screen, standing near her dad, especially the fat man eating a turkey drumstick.

She feared they'd all see she was a loser.

* * *

Her dad had worked as a millwright at BT Carbide & Service for over thirty years. He carried a toolbox. He never passed on overtime. Metal fillings dotted his skin, little gray spots under his eyes where the safety goggles ended and across his nose like blackheads. Old enough to retire but unable because of Jana's school, he sometimes worked seven twelves, coming home to eat dinner and pass out on the couch before starting again, new clothes but un-showered.

Jana knew she could have been a millwright, a good one, one who didn't miss the edges or smash the template, but her dad wanted better.

Nothing was better.

That was obvious now.

Jana ate another pill, crunched it between her teeth like something on a chalkboard she wanted erased. She swallowed and was unsure if the swallow worked.

Music would have helped, Van Morrison or Steve Miller, something mellow, or Kanye, some straight genius who knew facts and made everyone miserable.

The ceiling fan whirred and gave her focus.

The goth kid killed himself to Paul Simon.

Music had mostly sucked for a long time.

Maybe Trevor, the asscrack fiend, the man with the racecar hands, would hear the news of Jana's suicide and get his own ideas.

Maybe he'd bring flowers.

Maybe he'd ask before he touched.

One more pill, just to taste the dust.

When she tried to set the bottle down, it fell to the floor.

Jana was glad she hadn't cut her wrists, like she'd originally planned, like she'd imagined one night at Hoss's, staring at a steak knife. She didn't think she could do it. If she had done it, she would have gone too deep and messed it up.

Linda was a great friend.

Not everyone would have given up their oxycontin like that.

Maybe Jana would become an advisor. Maybe she'd go to another college, one far away with real professors and kind people, and get an education and come back and help kids who didn't know what they wanted to do, kids with moms in bathrobes and dads who worked until their nails were more grease than nails.

Jana would become an advisor and advise everyone to do good things.

"Don't spend money," she'd say, scream.

* * *

Her parents need not know. Plans had been implemented. Jana had called the hospital to make sure she wasn't considered a minor. "Just eighteen," she'd said when she was talking to the secretary at Presby. "Not twenty-one?"

That's why she'd told Linda not to give out her contact information.

Her parents were lovely people, even her mom.

She rubbed Jana's head when Jana couldn't sleep.

Jana couldn't tell if this was sleep.

Pretty soon Linda would be home.

She'd kiss Jana, friendly, not lez.

Linda would call the ambulance.

The ambulance would race here with its lights on.

Jana had forgotten to write the suicide note but that was okay. Linda would explain it. She would make up a story about Jana's sadness and how she broke into Linda's house and stole her pills and drank her beer and it would be a great story because it had to be and that was something Linda understood, like the Navy, do what needs to be done, the mission.

Bless me, Jana thought, I have done something brilliant.

* * *

Jana opened her eyes. She could no longer tell the difference between her lungs and the fan. It was slow and peaceful, all of it, like being drunk but without the drunkenness, especially her dad, how he projected into the room and gave love.

The paramedics, Jana knew, would be kind and understanding, they would drive safely and avoid potholes and give Jana an IV and they would be paramedics, who were angels, more or less, with community college degrees. They would believe everything, the lies that were true, the sadness that had been forced into Jana's body, the money that needed to be saved.

The paramedics would tell the nurses.

The nurses would understand.

They would bring Jana juice and blankets, they would take a minute to listen but Jana wouldn't say much because these were busy women, they were saints, they were savers of lives and dollars, they would mark Jana's charts, they would tell the doctors what the doctors needed to know, the doctors would mark other charts, they would be doctors, people not to be doubted, they would tell the shrinks, shrinks who were clueless, shrinks who were shrinks, and the shrinks would nod and tell the university their educated opinions and the university would nod and apologize, nod and bow, nod and give thanks, nod and check with their lawyers, lawyers who were afraid of suicides, of kids with ideas about death, and they would shit themselves and give Jana her tuition back, like she deserved.

Jana blessed them all, the saints of her dreams, and went to sleep.

Publication Notes

Some of these stories appeared in the following magazines (in different forms and sometimes with different titles):

Atticus Review, *Gulf Stream* (Florida International University), *Jenny Mag* (Youngstown State University), *Limehawk Literary Review*, *New World Writing* (formerly *Mississippi Review*), and *Referential*.

Many of these stories appeared in the U.K. in *Tears in the Fence*. Thanks to David Caddy, editor, for all his support.

Dave Newman is the author of seven books, including *The Same Dead Songs: a memoir of working-class addictions* (J.New Books, 2023) and *East Pittsburgh Downlow* (J.New Books, 2019). His collection *The Slaughterhouse Poems* (White Gorilla Press, 2013) was named one of the best books of the year by *L Magazine*. His poems, essays, and stories have appeared in magazines around the world, including *Ambit* (U.K.), *Tears In The Fence* (U.K.), *Gulf Stream, Belt,* and the legendary *Nerve Cowboy*. He appeared in the PBS documentary narrated by Rick Sebak about Pittsburgh writers. Winner of numerous awards, including the Andre Dubus Novella Prize, he lives in Trafford, PA, the last town in the Electric Valley, with his wife, the writer Lori Jakiela, and their two children. After a decade of working in medical research, he currently teaches in the Creative and Professional Writing Program at The University of Pittsburgh-Greensburg.

MORE ROADSIDE PRESS TITLES:

Innocent Postcards
John Pietaro

Cistern Latitudes
James Duncan

Another Saturday Night in Jukebox Hell
Alan Catlin

Abandoned By All Things
Karl Koweski

Ain't These Sorrows Sweet?
Lauren Scharhag

Gregory Corso: Ten Times a Poet
Leon Horton, Editor

She Throws Herself Forward to Stop the Fall
Dave Newman

We Don't Get to Write the Ending
Aleathia Drehmer

These Many Cold Winters of the Heart
Ryan Quinn Flanagan

Things You Never Knew Existed
Josh Olsen

Green Roses Bloom for Icarus
Hiromi Yoshida

Let the Scaffolds Fall
Shaun Rouser

Apocalypsing
Jason Anderson